THINGS I WISH
I'D KNOWN SOONER

ALSO BY JAROLDEEN EDWARDS

Harvest of Dreams
The Falcon Heart
The Chaldean Star
The Mountain of Eden
Wildflower
A Woman Between

THINGS I WISH
I'D KNOWN SOONER

Personal Discoveries
of a Mother of Twelve

~~~

JAROLDEEN EDWARDS

POCKET BOOKS

New York   London   Toronto   Sydney   Tokyo   Singapore

Portions of the book were previously published by
Deseret Book Company.

 POCKET BOOKS, a division of Simon & Schuster Inc.
1230 Avenue of the Americas, New York, NY 10020

ISBN: 0-671-55106-X

First Pocket Books hardcover printing May 1997

10   9   8   7   6   5   4   3   2   1

POCKET and colophon are registered trademarks of
Simon & Schuster Inc.

Text design by Stanley S. Drate/Folio Graphics Co. Inc.

Printed in the U.S.A.

Acknowledgments

With abiding gratitude . . .

To my parents, Charles and Julia Asplund, who taught me to love life, family, and the written word.

To my friends, cherished, but too numerous to mention, who have decorated and illuminated my life.

To my editor, Emily Bestler, who with her wit, creativity, wisdom, and profound insight has made my best much, much better.

To great writers whose words themselves are written in light.

To my blessed children, Marianna, Julia, Catherine, Charles, Christine, Robin, Carolyn, Weston, Robert, William, Jaroldeen, and Patricia, more precious than words, more valued than words can say, more dear than my heart can hold.

To my beloved husband, Weston Eyring Edwards, counselor, friend, adviser, enabler, supporter, teacher, lover, mentor, example—and all in all.

To all who have made my life so rich with joy—and who put up with this decidedly unfinished woman.

Contents

Preface

Let me say, right off the bat, that I do not know how to explain this book to you. It will not be crammed into a neat category. It is rather a strong-minded and impudent book and will not do as I tell it—somewhat like my twelve children.

It is not a book of essays. It is not a how-to book. It is not a book of philosophy or tidy answers to untidy questions. It is not an autobiography or a book of advice. It is not a book about housekeeping or child-rearing.

It is none of those things, exactly . . . and yet, it is all of these things—sort of.

I think this book could best be described as a book of conversations that we might have.

I love conversation. If you and I were to speak, our talks together would touch on the full spectrum of our lives—they would be intellectual, spiritual, funny, and personal. We would pass on quotes from other friends and share housekeeping hints . . . as a matter of fact, we would cover all of the glorious, myriad "stuff" (as Shakespeare called it) of which our dreams are made.

Women's conversations are, indeed, splendid things—diverse, profound, humorous, complex, and vivid. However, if women's conversations are splendid and diverse, it is only because they reflect that we, as women, are splendid and diverse.

The conversation of true friends, heard without envy, barriers, comparisons, or criticism, is good for the soul!

As I began writing this book, I remembered something my mother-in-law once told me. She was talking about her own mother, Caroline Romney Eyring, and she remarked, "My mother was not a very good cook—she was very impatient about food preparations. As a result of her impatience, however, the one thing she could make was wonderful pies."

I was a new bride when she said this. Her statement startled me because I had always regarded pie making as postdoctoral cooking. (As a matter of fact, I still do!) I could not see any possible relationship between a cook's impatience and the ability to produce something as complex and delectable as a pie.

"You see," Weston's mother went on to explain, "the less you handle pie crust, the more tender and flaky it is. A carefree cook who does not fuss or overwork her dough makes the best crust."

I think that what is true of pie crust is true of conversation as well. The more directly our thoughts come from our hearts, the more tender and true they will be to others.

So I have rolled out my pie crust. . . .

THINGS I WISH
I'D KNOWN SOONER

❧

The time to be happy is now,
The place to be happy is here,
The way to be happy is to make others so.

—ROBERT GREEN INGERSOLL

❧

1

Prime Time

I don't know why you would listen to somebody who missed her own prime! Because I did—I just plain missed it. I don't know if it occurred at two o'clock some morning when I was too busy rocking a colicky baby to observe it, or if it whizzed by me one day when I was dozing in a long PTA meeting, or if it sneaked past me while I was waxing the kitchen floor. Whenever and wherever it happened, I cannot tell you, but I do remember the *exact* moment when I recognized it had gone past me without my even noticing.

Like every other well-brought-up woman, I was raised to believe that life was a crescendo. Do everything right—eat your cereal, curl your hair, study, exercise, be sweet, and follow The Plan (although I was never too clear exactly what The Plan was)—and someday your life will be a success. You will reach

3

Happily Ever After and remain in that desirable—if somewhat nebulous—state for the rest of your life.

I confidently expected that there would come a time in my life when everything would be just as it was supposed to be—perfect. Of course, life kept getting in the way, but that didn't discourage me, since I knew that it would take a lot of years of effort and growth to reach the dreamed-of peak. I was patient— and besides, I was having an absolutely wonderful time on the way to getting there.

When my oldest child was ready to begin kindergarten, we lived in Harvard's student housing in Cambridge, Massachusetts, in the rather run-down but old-world charm of Holden Green. My husband was a graduate student at the university.

The townhouse-style apartments were filled with young couples like us, with lots and lots of children. It was a small, enclosed world of husbands who were graduate students and mothers who lived on pennies and cared for their babies. It was happy times and hopes and friendships and laughter and eyes filled with tomorrows.

When Marianna, our firstborn, was due to start kindergarten, we registered her in the Harvard preschool. It was a prestigious institution and we could barely afford the tuition, but we wanted her to have the very best. Since she was already the oldest of five children, we were determined to start this education business just right.

We lived in the heart of Cambridge, within walking distance of church and school, and did not have a car. I remember walking Marianna to school that first day. The September sun was like sifted gold, and the beech trees lining the narrow streets were radiant with the beginnings of autumn. Each magnificent old house along the walk was like a story waiting to be told.

I was pushing the stroller with the baby and my toddler in it, and the other three children skipped beside me. We were all full of sheer delight in the sights and sounds around us and the excitement of Marianna's first day of school.

When we got to the school, I stood outside for a moment and watched the other little ones arriving. Most of them were the children of wealthy professionals in the community. They were driven up to the school in Mercedeses and shining station wagons and sports cars. The other mothers, most of them, were women in their thirties and forties, with impeccably set hair, wearing beautiful suits from Peck and Peck and shining, expensive shoes. They all looked like magazine models to me.

I stood there with my children playing around my legs. My hair was windblown from the walk, and I was wearing jeans and sneakers. The baby's stroller looked the worse for wear, and I was frazzled from trying to keep my little ones out of the street and away from the cars. The contrast with those cool, controlled women was rather dramatic.

As I kissed Marianna good-bye and walked back home to put the other children down for their naps, I thought to myself, *It doesn't matter. Those are all older women — lots older than I am. Their husbands are well along in their careers. They don't have a lot of little children at home. They certainly aren't living on a student budget, and so they have time and money to spend on clothes and things. That's exactly how I'll be someday. In the meantime, I'm just going to enjoy being young and busy.*

Time passed. My darling daughter, Marianna, graduated from kindergarten, and later, my darling husband, Weston, finished graduate school. Through the years, we moved with Weston's work, from Chicago to Short Hills, New Jersey, to Los Angeles to Scarsdale, New York.

Two months after moving to Scarsdale our youngest child, Patricia, was born. I was in my early forties at that point, with twelve offspring, an old colonial house surrounded by apple trees, and all the children in the neighborhood in my front yard. Seventeen years had passed as quickly as though they had been one short autumn day.

It was time for school to start again, and I had another child beginning kindergarten. My high-school-age children drove themselves to school in their car, and I packed the remaining seven children into our blue family van. This battered, inelegant vehicle had taken Scouts camping, had been a moving van for countless young couples, had taken us on innumerable outings, and had driven across this vast country of ours more times than I cared to count. We had christened it "The Big Blue Bus."

We drove through Scarsdale to the lovely, English-style brick school, with its gentle draping of ivy. It was a glorious fall day, with the trees blushing red and gilded with yellow and the winding streets of Scarsdale lined with gracious homes.

I had been mopping the kitchen floor that morning and had hurriedly plucked the baby from her high chair for the drive to school. With the crying baby on my hip and two toddlers clinging to my legs, I took Robert, my first-day kindergartener, into the school to settle him in his classroom.

As I left the school to return home, I prepared to climb into the old blue van when something caught my attention. All around me I saw *young* mothers, in their twenties, bringing their immaculate children to school. They were driving Mercedeses and spanking-new Wagoneers. Their hair was shining and smooth and their clothes were country chic—calfskin loafers, pleated slacks, and expensive sweaters.

I stopped and looked down at myself. What had

happened? Somehow, somewhere, sometime along the way, I had become the *older* mother—the oldest mother there—and here I was, still in jeans and sneakers, with a slightly battered vehicle and young children clinging to my legs! Decidedly inelegant! And the *young*, perfect mothers looked like stars in those prime-time sitcoms with neat families.

Shaking my head, I looked at my three-month-old baby with a rueful smile as I buckled her into her car seat. She gave me a toothless grin, and a little dribble of milk ran down her chin. Her eyes were the color of the sky, and she looked at me as though she understood.

"Shucks, honey," I said with a philosophical shrug of my shoulders, "somewhere between Cambridge and Scarsdale I missed my prime!"

What made this moment so enlightening for me was the sudden realization that for years and years I had not even thought about the prime of life. My life had been so full of meaningful challenges, staggering amounts of work, unexpected learning experiences, complex relationships, and a growing focus and awareness of essential goals that my young, simplistic view of an ultimate ideal mold into which I would eventually fit had long since lost any validity.

With a wonderful burst of relief, I realized that I had grown free of that idealized image of uniform perfection.

The best thing I have discovered in adult life is that I have the privilege to choose my own patterns—to put first the things that matter the most to me and to my family.

Still, that day, I had to stop and ask myself honestly how much my sense of self and my list of priorities had been affected through the years by the expectations of a media-influenced society and by preconceived notions of the material things that would spell success in the eyes of other people.

Is our prime time only when gourmet meals are cooked? Is prime time only when we can afford Guess? jeans and a BMW? Is prime time only when our days follow a neatly prescribed pattern in our Franklin Day Planner? Is prime time only when our husband's job has an impressive title? Is prime time only when we have a career that is visible and important?

I do not think so. As a matter of fact, many of these things, fine as they are, can be barriers to what are really prime experiences. Outward measures of success reflect preconceived ideas put into our heads by society.

Real success can be measured only by ourselves— from within. We should never give up the right to choose in our own lives what we think is prime.

The difficult thing for women in creating a life that they can feel is prime is that they must make so many choices between things that are good. For example, it is a good thing to bake bread, have a job, read a book, go for a walk, do volunteer work, have a baby, or get a degree—but each woman must choose what is best for herself.

We cannot do everything, all the time, all at once. We can, through the years, do many things, at different times, one at a time. All those years, all those choices, and all those experiences can add up to prime time.

It is important for us to see our spectrum of choices as opportunities, not as frustrations. It is even more important to believe in our opportunity and responsibility to make those choices. Too often, we give up our right to choose in order to satisfy the expectations of others. When we go into debt to purchase something with the purpose of impressing others, we have let others make our choice. When we do that, have we created a moment of prime-of-success time—or have we created for ourselves months of stressful penury?

The irony is that when we evaluate our lives, some of the choicest times may be periods of sickness, poverty, and uncertainty, when all the deepest and most profound resources of our individual strength, our relationships, and our beliefs will be tested. The value of such times will be visible to no one but ourselves. Yet they will be prime times.

When we recognize our freedom of choice, we enter a stage of true personal discovery and the kind of freedom from worldly preconceptions that Sir Henry Bessemer, inventor of the process of steel making, exulted in when he said: "I had an immense advantage over many others dealing with the problem inasmuch as *I had no fixed ideas derived from long-established practice to control and bias my mind, and did not suffer from the general belief that whatever is, is right.*"

My wonderful conclusion on that long-ago day in Scarsdale, as I put my children to bed, kissed them good night, and looked at my rumpled, bumbling house full of things to do—some of which I loved doing and some of which I would put off as long as I decently could—was that I had not missed my prime at all.

Oh yes, I had missed that prime pictured in the magazines; I would never be elegant and svelte, never have coordinated towels (although I solve that problem in another chapter), a perpetually clean refrigerator, or coordinated children. But I had not missed my prime, my own personal, wonderful, wouldn't-change-it-for-the-world prime. I had been living it every day all through the years.

To anyone else, my life probably just looked noisy, confusing, untidy, and improbable, but the point is that no one else gets to place a value on our lives—no one but ourselves.

For me, all the years—even the hard ones—had been prime. Better than prime—choice!

Light from This Window:

လာ **W**hen we *live our lives dealing with things that really matter, the things that don't matter—don't.*

❧

Waste not your Hour, nor in the vain
pursuit
Of this and That endeavor . . .

— OMAR KHAYYAM

❧

2

A Full House

Preamble: It would be hard to explain to women who did not live through it what it was like to be a woman, a wife, and a mother in the 1970s. There was a harsh, divisive, strident movement in the ranks of feminism. Universities, television, newspapers, magazines, and highly visible "experts"—men and women—proclaimed that there were too many children in the world and that women should not be chained to home, husband, or babies. It was the "me" generation, with women crying "my turn" the loudest of anyone.

Zero population growth, the population boom, and *the feminine mystique* were all catch phrases under which a mix of genuine wrongs, personal angers, unproven theories, and divisive attitudes were packaged and sold to a questing generation of women.

There is no question that good came from this up-

15

heaval. Women's issues were brought out into the open and discussed, and many rights were established. New directions became possible. But, arguably, there are bitter legacies from that decade that linger still: a devaluing of children both in society and in personal lives, diminished respect for the traditional roles of women, divorce in epidemic proportions, and a polarization of men and women.

It was a time of what I like to call The Big Lie, when slogans masqueraded as ideas, and propaganda and emotion were disguised to look like thoughtful analysis. The task of homemaking and motherhood were demeaned as drudgery, while *jobs* were referred to as *careers* and glorified out of all proportion—certainly the idea of a career had very little relationship to the realities of most women's actual jobs.

Few women were able to refrain from being influenced by the pervasive antichild and anti–family role themes.

In the guise of freeing women, this movement was actually brilliantly forging new "manacles of the mind" (as John W. Gardner, the author of *Self-Renewal,* calls it). There are, of course, many ways to manacle minds, but none so clever as the catchy phrases disguised as responsible and established truth. It was a technique used effectively in the 1970's.

For example, almost always when writers or

speakers referred to the role of motherhood they would characterize it by the phrase "dirty diapers and dirty dishes." Now that's smart strategy. In a single phrase, they had captured two of the universally necessary but unappealing activities of mothering, had stripped motherhood to what they (and many others) considered to be its lowest common denominator, and by so doing had neatly denigrated the role and diminished mother and child by reducing their precious relationship to its most menial functions.

The strategy did not work on me because I already had a large family, and I did not know how I could send any of them "back." Besides, I understood that raising children meant infinitely more than any ridiculous catch phrase and I absolutely loved the experience of being a mother. I saw it as a profound career and a noble profession.

I also knew something about diapering a child that none of the slogan makers apparently did. As a matter of fact, if there is one thing in this world about which I am an expert, it is probably changing diapers. So, when I was confronted with this ad-campaign-level of thinking, I evaluated for myself what it *really* means to change diapers. *Is* it a demeaning activity for a Phi Beta Phi college graduate?

To begin with, there is no question that caring for an infant is a meaningful endeavor. Without the thoughtful, gentle care of a loving adult, babies die!

They die of starvation, disease, filth, and emotional neglect. There is absolutely no alternative. Babies must be cared for—and well cared for—or there is no continuation of life on this planet. A constant supply of the next generations—cared for, educated, and *alive*—is the single imperative of continued mortal existence. When we care for an infant, we are dealing with matters of actual life and death; there is nothing casual, demeaning, or unimportant in anything we do.

However, there is the matter of changing diapers—an inevitable interface of caretaker and child. In my analysis, I acknowledged that it can be a distasteful task, but also unquestionably one of service, of love, and of cleanliness.

Furthermore, there is a specific and genuine benefit to the task of diaper changing that elevates it to something quite wonderful. As anyone who has ever done it will attest, when you change a baby's diaper, it is necessary to look the baby squarely in the eye, to talk, to charm, to woo, to distract, to entertain—to do everything within your power to keep the baby contented, happy, and entertained while you perform the tricky maneuver. You have to be adorable and adoring to accomplish the task.

I observed that changing diapers requires a mother, several times a day, to interact directly with her baby, eye to eye, face to face, with all the charm she is capable of.

T. Berry Brazelton, M.D., a great pediatric authority, discovered a direct correlation between the effectiveness of mothers and the frequency of their eye-to-eye contact with their infants. Changing diapers is prime eye-to-eye time—several times a day, which goes to show that babies are very well designed creatures. They have a built-in mechanism for having their needs met.

Physically and emotionally, such daily activities as feeding, bathing, and diapering become the taproots of the lifelong relationship between mother and child. These functions constitute the "quality time" of infancy.

I have witnessed a mother diapering her baby and being so charming, adorable, vivid, and exuberant that she and the child rang with laughter as beautiful as the sound of golden bells. Only those who have never analyzed the real value and purpose of such activities can look at them with contemptuous eyes.

Some time ago, I was asked by the editors of a literary journal to write an essay on motherhood. America was in the thick of the women's movement at that time, and to be asked to write in praise of motherhood—especially motherhood in a large family—was a little like being asked to write an essay on democracy in mainland China today.

I had been a tournament debater in college, and

my natural instinct was to write an impassioned defense of motherhood. On point after point, I planned to trump my imagined adversaries. I wanted to win the argument.

As I wrote and rewrote the essay, I felt myself changing. I came to the firm conviction that I could not judge anyone else's ideas or values. Every person's opinions and thoughts are of import and should be respected. There is room in this world—and in our nation—for as many concepts and ways of life as there are people. I realized that in order to express my own point of view it is not necessary to change, correct, or demean another's.

In the end, I decided all I could do was write honestly about my own experiences and feelings and let readers take from my words whatever might be of value, truth, or help to them.

I simply wrote the account of a day in my life.

When the article was published, the editors wrote and told me that "people who read your essay either loved it or hated it—there was no in-between." (Did I mention that women were polarized in those days?)

Here is that day in my life:

I wake up in the morning to the sound of my husband's voice. But it is not really an awakening; rather, it is a continuing, for night as we used to know it no longer comes to our home. There is a lull in activity, yes; but in the way of our youth, when night and sleep were a total experience that blocked the chain of days, a precious all-in-one piece of unconsciousness, an ending and a forgetting—in that sense, night does not come. Even in sleep, there is a consciousness of caring, a wakefulness that tests the murmur of the house through the darkened hours. The hum of the refrigerator; a last dryer load of clothes with one clonking sneaker; water flushing; a cough; children padding on pajama'd feet through the always lighted halls; requests for drinks, solace from bad dreams, or a short diagnosis of unidentified aches.

Sometimes I open my eyes in response to an eerie sense of presence and see a face an inch from mine, staring—child standing, me lying, eye to eye. "I can't sleep," and then the blissful snuggle in. Or there will be a gentle rising to the surface of consciousness, a sudden awareness of silence, a listening . . . listening . . . listening . . . and settling back to rest in the wonder and reassurance of our burgeoned home.

Not yet six in the morning. My husband is shaving and calls over the running water—something from the train of his thoughts. He assumes that I am (a) awake and (b) fully aware of his mental preamble, even though he knows that we have an unspoken agreement: I never wake to the sound of an alarm, and he never wakes to the crying of a baby. He cannot resist this brief, empty piece of time. No more can

I, so I rouse and prop in bed and we continue the delicious conversation of our marriage. Fifteen minutes. Then up, making the bed, hair, slippers, robe, and a quick glance at our baby sleeping like a moist rose. Such beauty in our cluttered bedroom!

Morning husbands are so elegant. He comes from the dressing room in his starched white shirt, bright tie, polished shoes, face shining from shower and shave. All the beautiful odors, soap, shaving lotion, starch, and the masculine smell of his suit, mingle in that early morning embrace.

Breakfast with our high-school daughters is eggnog, toast, and orange juice. Never time for more. The girls hurtle into the kitchen, shoes in hand, long shining hair, books a-clutter, hunting for gym suits or brushes or pens. Their day fresh and new. I never get used to seeing them grown so tall and beautiful. I love their becoming, but I miss the little girls gone. It is a constant challenge to keep my relationship to them in the proper balance, since it must change and develop as they do. Too often, the childhood mother rises to the surface and makes a flat evaluation: "Change those stockings!" "Skirt's too short." "Take a sweater." "Do you have your homework and lunch?" Compromises reached, plans exchanged. As they fling out the door, with coats, books, and purses, I give each a brief kiss and a careful compliment, the ritual that says, "I love you. Hurry home."

Then one last apostrophe of time with my husband. Six-thirty A.M.—he looking like Brooks Brothers and me like the Earth Mother.

The next sweet half-hour is my own. It's gorgeous to read in a still-sleeping house, or spend quiet minutes with an early-awakened baby. At seven, I must be fully dressed with makeup and hair done, ready for the official day of the family to begin. The other children are wakened, first time cheerfully, second time firmly, and if a third time is necessary, sharply.

I dress the preschool children and babies in my bedroom. This bedroom is the hub of our home in the morning and evening. Here I keep a drawer with the stockings for the entire family. This serves two purposes. Naturally it saves a lot of sorting time, but it also makes it necessary for each child to come from the corners of the house to this room to complete dressing. I can make all the necessary checks—hair, teeth, clothes, homework, and morning chores. The stocking drawer is a siphon and it draws all the early morning family to me while I am busy changing diapers, tying shoes, and snapping trousers for the four youngest.

Breakfast and lunches are prepared with practiced swiftness. Simple meals. Bowls of hot cereal, milk, and oranges. Lunches crackling in brown paper sacks with each name in marker pen—Catherine, Charles, Christine, Robin, Carolyn. Sandwiches all the same ("Sorry you don't like cheese, Robin; I'll make peanut butter tomorrow." Carolyn says she doesn't like peanut butter and we all laugh. "Tuna on Wednesday!" I promise.), cookies, apples, and milk money. Gathered around the kitchen table, the children and I cram these last minutes with talking, facts, ideas, compliments, appointments, and schedules. Family prayer and momentary silence as they start to eat.

The clock is inexorable. So is the school bus. Again, at the door, the farewells. My cheek is kissed and I forget to wipe off the cereal and milk. Midday I will sometimes touch my cheek and find it still sticky.

Catherine's junior high starts late and so we do dishes and have a rare private talk. She practices flute or piano and then, long, dark hair bouncing, strides off to school. It would be wonderful to have twelve children and have each an only child.

Bless *Sesame Street*! That psychedelic learning feast! My three little boys sit in a rapt row. Fifteen minutes of hard exercise for me while they watch; the misery of middle age, many children, and all that car driving is that muscle tone is no longer inherent—it has to be earned.

I fill the sink to bathe the baby. It is a time of savoring. Maybe it has taken me all these children to appreciate how short these first months are. The glories of a new baby are beyond description. Hardly mortal! I revel in this tactile, subtle, exquisite, and complex experience. One unexpected bonus of motherhood is the visual beauty. I am enchanted by the sights of my children, the tones of skin, the clear eyes, the grace, the curve of hand and cheek, to see them racing across the back lawn in a certain slant of light.

At about ten o'clock, the baby is cared for and the discretionary part of the day begins. There is no one to tell me what I must do, only my own sense of responsibility and achievement. People often ask me how I manage with such a large family and I reply, "By a simple method of selective neglect." Which is just a way of saying that I manage through a system of compelling priorities.

My present life as a mother has three profound purposes. (This aside from the relationship with my husband, which is my dearest and consistent preoccupation.) The first is to fulfill all my obligations of love, as I understand them. The second is to educate my children—educate in the broadest sense, not just by helping them achieve skill and success in school, but by giving them a sense of awareness, responsibility, and joy. By far, the greatest amount of my time is spent in this endeavor. Third is my responsibility to give the best possible physical care to children and home. If any of these three purposes is neglected, the balance and richness of our family is impaired.

Basic order is essential. This to me means beds,

dishes, and general pickup must be done consistently and directly. Each child makes his bed on rising and clears his own dishes. Clothes washing is done early and late. Hurrah for the men who invented dishwashers, dryers, and Permanent Press! I am a compulsive picker-up and thrower-away; ask any child who has made the mistake of leaving a valuable piece of paper lying around. So the house is mostly neat. Once a week, the house is cleaned royally by the entire family. The rest of the time, no real cleaning except for accidents or VIP company.

Because the center of the day is too important to be expended on unenduring things, all the routine must be compressed into the early and late hours. Then we can spend the rest of the morning, my little ones and I, reading, doing projects, going to PTA meetings, visiting friends, gardening, or singing.

The pattern of life is greatly shaped by the houses in which we live.

This California house, with its open kitchen and adjoining family room and glass doors, is suited to supervising activities with my preschoolers and still working in the kitchen—preparing food, folding clothes, doing dishes, and so forth. My table is piled with papers, crayons, books, and glue. Along one wall are a blackboard and a bulletin board. Teaching is so much a part of my interaction with my children—so many to teach, so much for them to learn. "There are four seasons." "Rain happens this way." "Who is Abraham Lincoln?" "This is how you catch the ball."

I always try to hold at least one church or community job, not only because it is essential for my own spiritual, social, and developmental needs, but also as an example to the children. I love being involved, busy, serving in different ways. My young children often go with me to my meetings. They feel at home in the community.

At three o'clock, the children burst in from school and the house becomes vibrant with them. Imagine how many sheets of school assignments seven children bring home! We are inundated with smudged, gray, blue-lined papers. Practicing, homework, roller skating, friends, basketball, driving to lessons—and always talking, talking, talking. Ours is a noisy home.

At about seven o'clock, my husband returns. There is a crescendo of delighted welcome. He is the big event of the day. He makes his way into our bedroom with children clinging to his legs, pockets, and coattails. An audience congregates as he struggles into indestructible home clothes while he is assailed by simultaneous accounts of daily activities, demands for justice, homework problems, and general claims for attention. Those nights when he is gone (traveling or working or at meetings), the excitement is gone, too.

Supper is special because it is the one time we are

all together. My recipes are easy and served in stove-to-table cooking pots. I prepare meals with a minimum of utensils and time. The table is set by the children, with a red bowl filled with leaves or flowers and candles in the center—our nod to gracious living.

All the children are bathed each night. It is the easiest way to say, "That's the end of the day, my dears!" Our biggest bathroom is awash with clothes, shoes, sand, water, wet towels, and suds. After the little ones are storied to bed, the school-age children and I gather in a circle on the living-room floor. That is the theory, anyway. There is always a feeling of coming and going. We take turns reading a short chapter from an older children's book.

Thus begin the long good-nights. Suffice it to say that no one goes to bed without individual encouragement. Gradually the house begins to settle. "I have to finish this page." "My report is due tomorrow." "What shall I wear?" "I need another drink." "I forgot my prayer." Another round of kisses. "Good night. We love you." "Go to sleep." "Go to sleep." "Go to sleep."

When my husband is not traveling, we close the day as it began, sharing, laughing, discussing, recreating one another's enthusiasm, love, and joy. One last reassuring look in each room. We love you. We are here.

Precious commitment, eternal vigilance, limitless

caring: I think this is the essence of parenthood. We know its endless nature and live with a profound knowledge of the bitter cost if we fail.

Of course, not all days follow this pattern. Weekends are another world, and sometimes the whole system comes to a grinding halt. Illness, an unusual assignment, a child with a special need, or just an overwhelming day of weariness or frustration can destroy the whole chain. Sometimes I choose to ignore routine and steal a day for my own use. That is always the day visitors drop in. I wade through the toys, dishes, and children to greet my guests, knowing that they cannot see all the things I have done that day because what I have *not* done is so apparent.

It is an irony that motherhood is the one profession that a dedicated and educated adult can practice for a decade and still not be considered expert. Yet I confess I have confidence in myself and in my role. I believe I do it as well as I am capable of doing anything. I have chosen this life; it does not master me, I master it. I am not its victim, I am its recipient. And if there are times when I wistfully read a university catalogue, or wish that I could run instead of pushing a stroller and observing each leaf and stone, or get tired of the litany of no's and do this's, those times are not frequent and they just serve to confirm that life is a banquet, and, even when filled, we hunger and thirst.

So it is that each day runs its course, filled with being, many things undone, many just begun. And thus to bed . . . and a continuing into the night.

Light from This Window:

∽ *The time is so brief, we must make all of it count.*

Light—more light!

—LAST WORDS OF
WOLFGANG AMADEUS MOZART

3

An Illuminated Life

I was invited to accompany my husband on a business trip to Barbados and I was enormously excited. After all, it would be the first time I had ever been off the continent of North America and the first time I had ever been to an island. Pretty heady stuff.

The trip itself was not very glamorous. Our tickets from California involved several plane changes, with the final connection being made during a bitter snowstorm in New York. It was a long and arduous day of traveling on overcrowded planes across several time zones. It had been fourteen long hours since we had left our home at the crack of dawn. Still, I was shimmering with anticipation.

Travel-weary and disoriented, we finally arrived in Barbados.

My fantasy of a Caribbean island was a cross between the paintings of Gauguin and old movies starring Bob Hope and Dorothy Lamour. I had imagined palm trees swaying, the scent of frangipani (whatever that was), flowers, lush ferns, and the ocean lapping at my feet. I think I had expected to walk off the airplane like Dorothy walking into the Technicolor world of Oz. I wanted pure Hollywood fantasy with a little background music thrown in for good measure.

Instead, as we were herded off our airplane onto an open tarmac, all we could see was empty sky and other parked airplanes. The air was hot and muggy, and what little landscape we glimpsed was bare and flat.

We were hurried into the terminal, taken through customs, and then crowded into small English-made taxis. With luggage piled on our laps, we began a dizzying ride to our hotel.

Our taxi drove along a narrow, winding road (which I later learned ran down the center of the small island on the spine of its hilly crest) between tall stands of sugarcane ready to be harvested. For nearly an hour, we sped along, passing other taxis, seeing an occasional small house or a windmill, but for the most part, the tall, green cane fields banked the road and blocked our vision. It felt as though we were driving through a long, green tunnel.

When we arrived at our hotel it was not the large, colonial plantation–style building that I had envisioned sitting on a hill overlooking the ocean with a sweeping, palm-lined driveway. Instead, we drove into a small, intimate, flower-shaded courtyard, where we were greeted at the door of a vine-shrouded villa by a courtly gentleman.

Our host called a bellman, who took our bags and invited us to follow him down a twisting path that was overhung with flowering shrubs. The air felt much cooler in the scented shade of the overhanging flowers and trees, but we could see nothing except the shadow-patterned path in front of us. Even the sound of our footsteps was muffled. My sense of disorientation was profound.

The bellman opened the door to our cottage, and, as we entered, it sprang closed behind us. We stood blinking in the almost total darkness of our air-conditioned room. I could hear the bellman walking across the floor to the far wall, where he deposited our suitcases on some kind of a stand.

Confused, weary, and disillusioned, I stood by the door waiting for my eyes to grow accustomed to the darkness. The whole long day had been frustrating, and all that had sustained me was the dream of this wonderful place. But here I was! I had been in this paradise for over an hour, and all I had experienced was obscurity and disappointment.

Nothing was as I had dreamed it would be. Nothing made sense. Where was I? Supposedly somewhere on an island in the middle of an ocean—but at that point I was not sure either the island or the ocean really existed, and I was certainly in doubt about the whole "tropical paradise" thing! If there was an ocean, I surely had not seen it, except to fly over it!

Just then the bellman, somewhere by the opposite wall, pressed a latch. I heard a distinctive click, and then, with a dramatic sweep of his arms, the man threw open the floor-to-ceiling shutters we had not seen in the darkened room.

As suddenly as though a searchlight had been turned on, the room was bathed in a dazzling brilliance, and there, right before us, where only darkness had existed, was the huge, splendid tropical sun suspended on a horizon of burnished turquoise with the endless ocean waves beating below it.

Without even turning my head or changing the direction in which I had been looking, I could suddenly see not darkness, but the whole sapphire Caribbean stretching farther than my eyes could comprehend, with the froth of a lacy-white surf lapping up to the edge of our own personal, dazzling beach. All that glory not fifteen steps away! I just could not see it in the darkness. The glory had been there all the time, and I had not known it.

Our cottage's seaside wall was made entirely of glass. I had not been facing darkness, but a window onto eternity. I was just a breath from all I had dreamed and I had not even guessed it. Light made all the difference.

Illumination—that is what our lives are all about —those brief moments in the darkness and confusion of our daily experience when a word, a thought, an action suddenly throws open the shutters, and for a brief instant, through an uncovered window, we see not the shadowed and confusing tunnel of our mundane days, but, in a splendid flash of light, a glimpse, a portion, of forever.

Light from This Window:

༐ *Understanding and truth are often with us, in our very own rooms. When moments of sudden enlightenment occur, we should celebrate them, learn from them, record and remember them. Because as surely as the shutters open, they will close again.*

Flower in the crannied wall,
I pluck you out of the crannies,
I hold you here, root and all, in my hand,
Little flower—but if I could understand
What you are, root and all, and all in all,
I should know what God and man is.

—ALFRED LORD TENNYSON

4

Magic Windows
of Light

I have always felt that although the circumstances of individual lives may be dramatically different, still, in meaningful ways, we are all much alike. Those things we have in common are far greater than those things that divide us.

The most common characteristic shared by ordinary people is that each one has an individual life that is splendidly unique and in some wonderful and mysterious way, extraordinary. It is a marvel that we are all both ordinary and extraordinary at the same time.

Knowledge and understanding are the real treasures of existence, and we become grateful for our own life, even with all of its limitations, pain, and challenge, when we begin to appreciate the fact that it is the tool by which we learn. Each life yields truth

41

in its own way. Molecular structure can be learned from a daisy or from a snail.

Thus it is that the mother in Lapland who gently rocks her child to sleep shielding his eyes from a never-setting sun, the Bedouin mother who feeds her child goat's-milk yogurt in the blazing heat, the Andean mother who straps her child close to her body so he may sleep as she climbs the mountain path in the thin, cold air—thus it is that each one is learning the identical concept of love. Each is looking at the same view, but seeing it through a different window.

I remember vividly the day my eighth child was placed in my arms. Why then? Why the eighth child? Why didn't I know or experience this with my first child? We have no idea why moments of learning take place when they do. What was it about this particular birth—this particular child—that caused me to suddenly comprehend a truth that could not be put into words? I don't know. This remarkable window of understanding simply did not open until my eighth baby was born. Perhaps I was not ready to see it until then.

It was not a new thought or a new feeling. I am sure many mothers have known it before me, and many more will comprehend it after. It was an insight both sudden and true, one that I perceived in an instant, unexpectedly, so profoundly that I shook with the knowledge of it.

As I held my new baby, he opened his eyes and looked at me, and in that perfectly ordinary moment, deep within his eyes, as though I were actually looking through a window or a telescope, I suddenly saw the whole sense of eternity. I saw ourselves and our relationship, and our relationship beyond time and place. I gasped.

I cannot describe it any better than that. I suddenly knew something I had never known before. I saw, for a moment, a glimpse of who we really are.

For a brief instant, in the direct and silent intelligence of those brand-new eyes from which gazed a spirit as everlastingly old and young as my own, I saw a microcosm of the love of God, the mature soul in that infant's body, and the truth of our eternal nature. I felt I had been privileged to look through my child's eyes to see a glimpse of heaven. For just one brief instant, all the walls had fallen away.

Later that night, I wrote the following words:

A child's eyes are the cathedral of a mother's soul:
Through them she worships flawlessly.
In them she sees eternity.

Knowledge may come in many ways, but it is those sudden, unexpected moments of insight that particularly intrigue me, those moments in our questing when a veil is suddenly torn from our eyes and we see clearly.

The principles of physics have always existed, since the creation of the world, and are demonstrated daily in the natural workings of the earth. Through the centuries, how many apples, do you suppose, have fallen right in front of people's eyes—and yet no one has really seen them falling? Not really *seen* what was happening, what forces are at work.

Isaac Newton observed a falling apple with a vision that somehow penetrated the simplicity and dailiness of that event, and because he truly *saw*, the laws of physics were discovered, and the world was changed forever. Newton identified a truth that had always been there, just waiting to be seen with illuminated eyes.

It is some of these glimpses of surprised light in my own life that I would like to share with you in this book.

James Joyce called such moments *epiphanies*. I rather like that word. It has a rich, important sound to it—and a touch of exaltation as well.

A word like *epiphany* cannot take itself too seriously because it has a kind of homely sound, like *piffle* or *funny*—which is appropriate, because moments of enlightenment can be pretty down-to-earth and humorous.

Epiphany literally means a flash of pure insight—

one of those rare moments when everything coalesces to create an instant of total comprehension.

So there you are! A simple flower can unlock the secrets of the universe. Things of great importance can be revealed in the humdrum. The extraordinary can be manifested in the most ordinary of places, like a kitchen.

I have gathered, like a bouquet of memory, some of the moments of epiphany in my ordinary yet unexpected life. I hope the fragrance of these memories may bring to your own mind the wisps of past remembrance when, for the briefest of seconds, you, too, have caught glimpses of something truer and larger than anything you ever dreamed.

Light from This Window:

ᖚ *Out of the simplest moments of our lives can come extraordinary flashes of insight, knowledge, and wisdom. The most ordinary things can become windows of light.*

This time, like all times, is a very good one
if we but know what to do with it.

— RALPH WALDO EMERSON

5

A Little Bit Here, a Little Bit There

It was a bleak, rainy day and I had no desire to drive the two hours from the warmth of the beach to the cold mountaintop at Lake Arrowhead where my daughter lived.

A week earlier, she had called and insisted that I must come to see the daffodils that some woman had planted at the top of the mountain. I had promised. So, on a gray, foggy March morning, I was reluctantly making the journey; I almost stopped and turned back when I saw the mountains shrouded in clouds.

Had I known how thick the fog would become on the winding road toward the summit, I would definitely have turned back, but by the time the mists had swirled in around me, it was as far to go back as it was to go forward, so I inched my way up the perilous Rim of the World Highway until I finally turned off at the road to my daughter's house.

"I am not driving another inch!" I announced as I entered, hugging my two little grandchildren. "I will stay and have lunch, but as soon as the fog lifts, I'm heading back down the mountain."

"We drive in fog all the time," Carolyn said nonchalantly.

"I don't care," I retorted. "I am not going back onto that road to see daffodils or anything else!"

"But I do need you to drive me to the garage to pick up my car," Carolyn said. "Could we do that at least?"

"How far is the garage?" I asked cautiously.

"Just about three minutes," she answered. "I'll drive. I'm used to it."

We got back into my car, and Carolyn drove. After about ten minutes, I looked at her anxiously. "I thought you said it was three minutes away."

Carolyn grinned. "We're taking a detour."

I was being kidnapped by my own daughter! We were back on the road along the crest of the mountain, and the fog still surrounded us like thick veils. *Nothing could be worth this,* I thought.

Just then, we turned off the main road and twisted down a narrow track into a parking lot beside a little stone church.

Getting out of the car, Carolyn indicated a path.

The fog was beginning to lift a little, and gray, watery sunshine was trying to peek through.

The path we followed was thick with old pine needles. Huge, black-green evergreens towered over us, and the mountain sloped sharply away on the right side, dotted with clumps of live oak and mountain laurels. Gradually, the peace and silence of the place began to fill my mind.

Just then, we turned the corner of the path, and I stopped—dead stopped—and literally gasped in amazement. There before me was a most incredible and glorious sight! So unexpected and unimagined.

From the top of the mountain, sloping down several acres across folds and valleys, between the trees and bushes, following the natural flow of the terrain, were rivers of daffodils in radiant bloom. Every color of the spectrum of yellow—from the palest ivory to the deepest lemon to the most vivid salmon-orange—blazed like a carpet before us.

It looked as though the sun had tipped over and spilled gold in rivulets, splashing down the mountainside. In the center of this field of wild color, there cascaded a waterfall made of purple hyacinth. Throughout the garden were little meditation platforms with barrels of coral-colored tulips. And, as if this bonanza of color were not enough, over the heads of the daffodils, Western bluebirds darted and frolicked, their magenta breasts and sapphire wings like a flutter of jewels.

My writer's mind was filled with a riot of questions: Who created such beauty—such a magnificent garden? Why? Why here in this out-of-the-way place? Why a garden that blooms for only a few weeks each year? *How?*

As we approached the mountain home that stood in the center of the property, on a front deck we saw a poster, which was titled: ANSWERS TO THE QUESTIONS I KNOW YOU ARE ASKING.

The first answer on the poster was: ONE WOMAN—TWO HANDS, TWO FEET, AND VERY LITTLE BRAIN. The second answer was: ONE AT A TIME. The third answer was: STARTED IN 1958.

We walked in that maze of beauty with the children and felt we had come to some rare and wondrous place.

"She's still at it, you know," Carolyn told me. "The woman who lives here. Every year, she finds a new species of daffodil and plants a new section."

As we drove back home, I was silent. I was so moved and in awe of what we had seen I could scarcely speak. "She changed the world," I finally said. "One bulb at a time. That's the only way this garden could be accomplished. There are no shortcuts to something like this. Just think. She started forty years ago. Just one bulb at a time. Probably just the beginning of an idea, but she kept at it and at it. And the world is forever different and better because of her vision and her years of consistent effort. One bulb at a time," I repeated.

The wonder of it would not let me go. Finally, I sighed.

"Imagine. If I had had a vision all those years ago and had worked at it, just a little bit every day for all those lost years, what might I have accomplished?!" My voice was full of regret.

Carolyn laughed at the pointlessness of my remorse. She looked at me sideways, still smiling. "Start tomorrow," she said with wisdom and cheer. "Better yet, start today!"

Light from This Window:

തര *We can change the world, just one bulb at a time—and it adds up to something wonderful.*

❧

So wise so young, they say . . .

—WILLIAM SHAKESPEARE

❧

6

The Cookies

I used to triple my cookie dough recipes, and it would take me a whole afternoon to bake them all. I would keep both ovens busy, putting in double cookie sheets, then removing the batches, taking off the hot cookies, forming the new ones, placing the batter on the sheets, and putting the next load back into the ovens to bake.

One day I asked Catherine, who was about thirteen years old, if she would bake the cookies for me since I had to go to a meeting. She was happy to accept the assignment. I left her with the huge bowl of dough and expected I would be home before she had finished baking half of it.

When I returned an hour and a half later, the table was lined with fresh dish towels and perfect cookies, beautifully arranged, were cooling along its entire expanse. I was astonished at how quickly my daughter had moved the cookies through the process. She was taking the next-to-last batch of cookies out of the oven, and as I watched, I soon discovered her method.

As sheets of cookies baked in the oven (a time during which I usually fidgeted or was pulled away on another chore—often burning the cookies because of lack of attention), Catherine was busy placing waxed paper on the counters and spooning out individual pre-formed cookies. The minute she removed a cookie sheet from the oven and lifted the baked cookies onto the clean towels to cool, she rapidly picked up the already formed cookies from the waxed paper, and in a minute had popped the cookie sheet back into the oven. There was no downtime in the process at all. She had the four cookie sheets rotating in the two ovens constantly, and her own time was continuously and effectively used.

Watching the simplicity of her solution and the smoothness with which she completed her work, I knew I had learned not only how to bake cookies better, but also an important principle upon which to base my approach to all of my habitual, ongoing tasks.

Light from This Window:

∽ *Almost everything we do can be done more effectively and efficiently if we pause to analyze it with fresh and creative thinking.*

The known is finite, the unknown, infinite. We stand on an islet in the midst of an illimitable ocean. . . . Our business in every generation is to reclaim a little more land.

—THOMAS HENRY HUXLEY

7

Things I Wish I'd Known Sooner

When my husband was graduating from Harvard Business School, on the last day of classes, General George Doriot, one of his professors, invited students to bring their spouses to his final lecture. During the hour and a half in which we sat in the amphitheater of Baker Hall listening to General Doriot, we heard a most astonishing collection of advice, wisdom, and personal observations gathered by this remarkable man through a long career of achievement and distinguished business and political connections.

General Doriot did not attempt to connect his bits of advice or give them a pattern. He merely said, "These are some things a successful man should know and do." I remember distinctly his words, delivered in his elegant, French-accented English. "You will take three newspapers wherever you live: the *Wall Street Journal* because you cannot succeed in business without its information, your local newspaper because you must be informed about the community in which you live, and the *New York Times* because it is the most brilliant paper written."

Then he pulled out a copy of the *Times* and said, "Now I will teach you how to read a newspaper so that you will not look undignified, you will not make undo fuss or noise, and you will not get your hands dirty. You must always read the *New York Times* obituary section first because only the lives of significant people are reported there. If you read how they succeeded, you will be more able to succeed yourselves."

General Doriot then proceeded to show everyone in the room how to read a newspaper neatly, crisply, efficiently. For many years when we lived in the suburbs of New York and commuted by train to Manhattan, I was struck with the difference I noted between people who knew how to handle a newspaper well and those who struggled, rattled, and crumpled. General Doriot was right! The ones who knew his "method" looked more composed, and yes, successful.

Many other pieces of advice, as specific and seemingly trivial, were shared: thoughts on dressing, on interviewing, on how to take vacations, on how to eat a business lunch. Each idea was little more than a snippet of advice, and yet each one was applicable to the real lives and challenges these bright budding executives were soon to face.

Years later, perhaps most of those students would be unable to recall their classes on business theory and accounting techniques, but most of them would still remember General Doriot's advice on pocket handkerchiefs and what to order at a business lunch (fish, because it is easy to chew and swallow, and thus you can talk more freely).

It has occurred to me that there are many things I have learned that could have improved the quality of my life had I known them earlier. So perhaps I, like General Doriot, will share some of these scattered bits of knowledge.

I believe it is essential for every woman to recognize that one of her most important roles in life is the creation of a home. This is a cherished gift we can give, both to ourselves and to others. In a lifetime, we will create many homes, beginning with the influence we exert in our childhood homes and the memory and perception of that home that we carry with us into adulthood. We must learn self-esteem and self-motivation so that wherever we are we are at home with the person we are and feel comfort and security within that person.

Finally, we need to create our physical home, the four walls and roof within which we live and where we have the opportunity to build something wonderful, something intangible, something that gives a sense of welcome, order, love, and vitality, something that becomes a true home. Whether we live in a one-room studio, a basement apartment, a small tract house, or a stately manor does not matter; the creation of a home within those walls is a demanding challenge. It is a challenge I have faced eighteen times in my marriage.

I have been in great mansions and have felt the cold, hollow echo of rooms where no home existed— only a collection of things. I have been in other magnificent residences where a loving and caring person with generosity and warmth has created the sweetness of a cottage. I have been in small apartments where friends have welcomed me with such graciousness and love that I have felt I was in Eden—and did not want to leave.

From the cluttered, sparsely furnished starter house of a young family to the quiet, memory-filled two-room apartment of an elderly, valiant mother, in each place there is a remarkable and unique feeling of home, created by a remarkable and unique woman.

If we succeed in creating that subtle miracle called a home, it will become the bedrock that gives substance, meaning, and purpose to life. Home is the beginning and will be the thing that stands, cherished, productive, and valued, long after job changes, mergers, economic cycles, and retirement. Even though the location of our house may change, the four walls may come down, the rooms may shrink from ten to three, our "home" can remain intact wherever we are.

Married or single, parent, professional, student— whatever the circumstance of our life, we can create an environment that will bless our own life and the lives of others. In ancient England, Gothic cathedrals were called the pillars of the earth. The homes we create today are the pillars of heaven; they are also the pillars of our society. Winston Churchill said it well when he said, "We create our homes and then our homes create us." What we are, as individuals and as families, is reflected in our homes, measured by our homes, and established in our homes.

Homemaking does not need to be the only thing we do. Many excellent homemakers are productive in far-flung activities and professions, but the priority of creating places of *belonging* must remain. Without homes where values are learned, emotions are acknowledged, people are cherished, and joyous times are created, our society, as we know it, becomes a shadow.

Since the functioning of homemaking is undervalued by the world today, women must comprehend, as primary makers of homes, the significance of the task and confirm for themselves its importance. Inner conviction and knowledge of truth are the great motivators. There may be times when frustrations, loneliness, weariness, other responsibilities, and lack of support will rob the task of its satisfactions and cloud our understanding, but we must never lose our inner conviction of the importance of what we are doing when we create a home.

I wish I had understood this, clear to the marrow of my bones, much sooner.

Recently while attending some business meetings in Chicago with my husband, I went to a museum with the wife of a prominent mortgage banker. She is a woman whom I admire and like a great deal. She has character, charm, education, wit, and a wonderful sense of self.

Polly was raised in New England and lived there with her husband for many years. Recently she had moved to the Southwest because of her husband's work. With typical flair, good cheer, and optimism, Polly had accepted this upheaval in her life. Almost immediately upon moving, she set herself the task of designing and building a home. When the house was completed, it was a place of warmth and beauty, a contemporary adaptation of a New England colonial, with fireplaces, high ceilings, and a spacious entrance hall—everything designed to welcome and embrace, not to impress. She furnished the home with antiques collected by generations of her family, including a mahogany dining-room set made by her great-grand-father, a New England cabinetmaker.

The home was as charming, appealing, lovely, and impressive as Polly herself. But the thing that made her home unique was shown by the way she put together the open house she held as soon as it was completed. It was a great party, brimming with flowers, food, music, and conversation. Polly invited all of her wide circle of old and new friends, including business associates, neighbors, fellow volunteers from various charity organizations with which she was involved, members of her book club, grocery-store clerks, her doctor and dentist, and many others with whom she came in contact.

Also included in the party were the men who had helped to build the house. These men were the honored guests, from the ditchdiggers to the painters, the carpenters, the men who installed the carpets, the plumbers, and the electricians. She knew them all by name, knew their wives and children, and welcomed them with open arms. As she introduced these people with gratitude and warm affection, Polly commented, "This is really their house, you know. They made it. Without them, it wouldn't exist."

As we rode to the museum that day, Polly and I talked about many things. Assuming that a woman with Polly's resources must be involved in some impressive endeavor, I asked, "Well, now that your new home is finished and your youngest son is off to college, what new challenge are you going to take on?" (I know now how many false assumptions are contained in that question.) Polly sat quietly for a moment, then turned to me with a smile and a slight shrug of her shoulders. What she then said pierced me to the quick. It was a moment of insight that I believe every woman should experience.

"I just want to keep doing the most important thing, the thing that I love above everything else," she said. "I just want to keep finding ways to do it better. All my life, for the rest of my life, I want to keep being the finest wife, the most loving and caring mother—and, I hope, someday, grandmother—it is possible to be. To me, nothing else holds a candle to this in terms of satisfaction and importance. Anything else I do is just my way of saying thank you for the privilege of being a mother."

I was overwhelmed by the strength and depth of the conviction of this sophisticated woman of the world. She is a prime mover in the city in which she lives, but she knows exactly what is important and of value to her, and nothing shakes her from that focus.

Thus I was taught something I wish I had known sooner: to never apologize for or waver in the joy and dedication of what I do or let other voices deter me from a straightforward, inner sense of value and commitment.

The following list of things has very little pattern or organization, since most of them came to me as unexpectedly as all my other windows of light. I recognize that these are personal insights and some of them may be things that apply only to my own life, but they serve as examples of how we learn from our personal lives and of the varieties of insight that can come through individual experiences. So here we go!

LESSON 1 ᨳ

Have a credit card for identification purposes only. Use it sparingly. Don't even call it a "credit" card; call it an "identification" card. Lives can quickly become enmeshed in indebtedness and bondage when a credit card is used as though it were money. If we do not have the money to pay for an item this month, what makes us believe we will have the money next month—unless we consciously save it? It is too easy to flip out the card and buy anything we desire. Often, the thing we have bought will be used up or worn out long before the debt is paid.

LESSON 2 ᨳ

Save at least a little money every month. Even a few dollars a month can make a difference. One of the greatest satisfactions in life is to watch a savings account grow. It is somewhat like dieting. At first we love watching the progress; then we hit plateaus when we think we will never reach the next goal. A sudden emergency can deplete the hard-earned total, and the process begins again. However, it is the *process* that is important. Clark Hinckley, a banker, advises that if we are in debt, we should save rigorously (paying the interest on the debt) until we have saved twice the amount of the debt. Then, as soon as possible, we should pay the debt in full. The reason for this is so we will still have savings left and therefore maintain our incentive to save. We need to save for self-discipline, save for security, save for freedom. The amount does not matter; the principle does—at least that is what I have come to believe.

LESSON 3 ᴼᴬ

Try to live within or even below your means. A wise woman in a suburb of New York City, a person who could have afforded the most expensive home in town, lived in a small, attractive, frugal house, drove a modest car, dressed simply, and was by far the most successful real estate executive in the area. One day she said to me, "You know, Jaroldeen, it is what you keep, not what you make, that makes you wealthy." Her quiet generosity to countless others, distributed from her wisely managed wealth, gave her far more personal satisfaction than any showy display of money could possibly have done.

LESSON 4 ᏩᎨ

Learn to manage your money—don't just spend it. I wish I had learned earlier to do without longer. An empty room is better than one filled with hurriedly bought junk. If I had known then what I know now, I would have waited longer and bought better things that would last a lifetime. I wish I had realized that space in a home does not need to be filled. Open rooms are pleasant, especially when children are small. Undraped rooms and uncarpeted floors can be fresh and bright and very livable, especially when children are toddlers. One quality piece of furniture is worth several that will be discarded.

LESSON 5 ᏩᎨ

Have at least one well-made, attractive, conservative outfit to wear whenever it is necessary to meet business or professional groups. Had I learned this lesson earlier, it might have saved me many frantic, last-minute, and numerous unwise purchases. In the early years of my marriage, I was careful to see that my husband had a good-quality wardrobe, one appropriate to his work. This was not an extravagance; we felt that it was important if he was to succeed in the business world. I now realize that it is important for women who are at home full-time to understand that they need to have at least one outfit in which they will feel comfortable and well dressed in any setting. It is important for self-esteem as well as for practical purposes. A great-looking, great-fitting black dress that speaks of quiet sophistication can hardly go wrong in any setting. It is worth every cent.

Conversely, a professional woman should have at least one or two outfits that look appropriate at nursery-school programs or at a soccer game to help her look like a mother and not, as a friend of mine says, "like someone on a ten-minute break from a marketing meeting."

It is false humility and poor economics not to have appropriate clothes.

LESSON 6 ᴏᴡᴏ

Make your home, no matter how modest, as lovely as possible. Discover for yourself the gracious touches that are possible and important to you in your own particular circumstances. For the first ten years of our marriage, my husband was a student. Until he obtained his doctorate, we lived in truly meager conditions. We had six children when he received his degree from Harvard, and we had lived in student housing on limited funds for all those years, but my memory of that time is that we lived in comfort and style. This is because I learned to enjoy inexpensive "luxuries." Rolls of ribbon purchased at a discount house, a spray of parsley in a cup on the kitchen windowsill, jelly beans in a pretty jar, candles on the dinner table, a paper-lace doily under a plate of homemade cookies, and lemon oil gleaming on scarred wood all give the feeling of peace, beauty, and plenty.

LESSON 7

Learn early the principles of order and cleanliness. *Details make the difference.* Shiny windows and glass doors with fingerprints rubbed off, showers that are scrubbed, floors that shine, a front door that is freshly painted—these are some of the things that make a home look valued and cared for. We need to focus our efforts. Often we don't need to dust everything; just dusting the coffee table regularly will give the feeling of order to the living room. Above all, I have learned and relearned that clutter is the enemy of order and sanity. I wish I had learned earlier to sort, discard, and organize. Declutter constantly.

LESSON 8

Buy white linens and white towels. I learned this after years of making ten beds and cleaning four to five bathrooms a day and sorting tons and tons of laundry. When we visited the Plaza Hotel in New York City, I noticed that every piece of linen was white. A window of light! Of course! No sorting. I could use bleach in every load and keep white towels looking like new. No more faded rose, dingy blue, blurred designs, trying to sort darks and lights—in fact, no more sorting at all! All my linens could go in the same load of wash! And nothing is so elegant or matches every bathroom and bedroom decor so well as white. No more trying to match the striped sheets, or the Flintstone pillowcases, or the green towels, or giving up in despair and putting the pink flowered top sheet with the navy plaid fitted sheet. It took many years to phase out my old linens, but every time I see a white sale or need to replace old and worn linens, I buy white. The result has been a lessening of work and an increase in beauty in my home.

LESSON 9 ⁓

Learn to prepare food with an aesthetic sense of its beauty, texture, and possibilities. I learned this far too late. For years, without household help, I prepared meals for fifteen people daily. Then I attended a memorable cooking class. The long table at the front of the room was covered with a lovely plaid cloth, and on it were displayed beautifully arranged baskets filled with many varieties of apples. The woman who taught the class spoke to us of the miracle of apples, described the different varieties, and demonstrated how to prepare several apple dishes. As I watched her hands caress the fruit and create pies, strudels, and dumplings, I suddenly saw the preparation of food in a whole new light. It was an act of artistic creation, a spiritual, tactile, and visual feast. Each apple had become a precious jewel. That vision has not left me.

In summary, I wish I had understood much earlier that home is not a thing to be looked at. It is not something we create to impress others. It is not an object. Home is a living, breathing thing—a laboratory for living. I believe we should each create a home that makes people think, *I want to be* in *that home,* not *I wish I* owned *that home.*

And finally, I would like to share two things that I learned soon enough, and I have practiced them as well as I could all of my life.

The first of these discoveries is that I have *loved* raising children. Even the challenges—and there have been many—have given me abiding joy mixed with the sorrow and pain. A friend who had experienced the most tragic event a parent could live through said to me, "Even knowing the end from the beginning, I would not have missed one moment of it." That is how I, too, feel. I do wish, though, I had known from the first moment of parenting what my father-in-law taught me. "Let 'yes' be your natural response rather than 'no,'" he counseled. I would like to have learned earlier to want to serve more as my children's "facilitator" and less as their "controller."

The other discovery was an early one: I have known from the moment my life joined my husband's that my greatest joy would come from loving and supporting him and involving myself in his life. Our relationship and our functions within it change as the circumstances of our life change, but the priority is constant. We are committed to each other, and we have spent our lives together feeling that we are each involved completely in the cares, concerns, and responsibilities of the other. With patience and interest, he has explained his career to me and has allowed me to feel knowledgeable and aware of its many exciting and demanding challenges. In the same way, I have woven him into the life of our home, even with his extensive travels and long, long hours of work, so that our children have felt his presence when he has been away, and he has been completely aware of their concerns and activities.

We are a very normal family. We have done some things well and we struggle to overcome our faults and difficulties, but we are joined together by love, and we each do our part toward achieving our common goals.

What I have learned is perhaps best summarized in an experience we had a few years ago. We were living in Los Angeles, and my husband came home one Saturday after some early meetings and said, "Let's go kite flying."

Off we drove to the Santa Monica beach, about an hour's drive. We sang favorite family songs in the car and laughed and talked. When we arrived at the beach, we stared in disbelief at the ocean. There was hardly a wave on the surface. The air was hot and muggy, and, for the first time in our memory, not so much as a breath of air was coming across the water. The children got out their kites and ran, huffing and puffing, along the beach, but the kites simply dragged in the sand. They turned to their father with disappointment in their faces, suddenly as listless as the kites.

"There has to be wind somewhere in Los Angeles," Weston said with conviction and enthusiasm. "Get back in the car and we'll find it." So all fourteen of us piled back in.

Through the long afternoon, we drove through the streets of Los Angeles, stopping at parks and open lots. No wind. But we never lost heart. Weston was at the wheel and I poured my energy into the time we spent in the car, telling stories, pointing out the sights, laughing, talking, singing. At last, late in the afternoon, we arrived at Griffith Park.

"There it is," my husband said, pointing upward, "the highest point in the city. There must be some wind up there!"

And so we climbed up the highest hill in the park. There, perched on the very roof of the city, overlooking the park, the planetarium, and the great stretches of streets, houses, and skyscrapers, we clung to the narrow summit of the treeless mountain and felt the gentle updraft of warm air. My husband took the ball of string and played one of the kites into the air. The soft breeze caught the bright wings of the kite and carried it upward, and we all stood together on the crowded hilltop, holding one another and smiling upward as it flew bravely into the sun.

Light from This Window:

୶ *When we know what we are searching for, and if we refuse to give up, there will be many times when we will be privileged to find the lift of rising air, and oh, how our kites will soar!*

The Seed however broadcast will catch
somewhere and produce its hundredfold.

—THEODORE PARKER

8

Wildflower Seeds

For many years, we lived in Connecticut in a wonderful house that looked like a converted barn, with a lawn in the front and a back yard of natural woods. Brambles of wild blackberries and rhododendron bushes were hidden in the tangled growth, while volunteer wisteria vine trailed the front of our fence. Old, moth-eaten dogwood trees lined the road and the stone fence that fronted the property.

We loved that house, the village, our neighbors, and the glorious display of nature as each season tried to outdo the others. It was impossible to choose a favorite time of year. Spring, with daffodils blanketing the clear fields and rimming the houses, the fresh green fuzz on the dark branches of the trees that arched over the narrow, winding roads, and the balmy, ocean-scented breezes coming across Long Is-

land Sound. Summer, with its deeply shaded wood-
lands, the sun filtering through the rustling leaves, the
lush lawns and exuberant growth of vine, bush, and
flower, and the hot, lazy afternoons. Autumn, unre-
strained, lavish, a kaleidoscope of colors too brilliant
and vibrant for the eye to hold, prodigal in harvest
and in beauty. Winter, with the gentle silence of falling snow, blue, silver, and white, winds that chased
us indoors to the sweet warmth of a crackling fire.
Who could choose a favorite season from these boun-
ties?

In such surroundings, the symbiotic relationship
of man and nature becomes very strong, and as a result, I spent a great deal of time in the local nursery
and garden shop, looking for something to grow, either indoors or outdoors, depending on the season. It
was there that I bought my first flower bulbs, and I
watched with maternal joy as the tulips, daffodils,
and jonquils sprang from the earth the following
spring. It was there that I learned that zucchini will
grow when nothing else in the world will.

It was there that I discovered, for my indoor winter plants, the wonders of Aspergis fern, Reiger bego-
nias, cyclamen, grape hyacinth, and paper-white
narcissus for Christmas, and a massive wreath of
dried bay leaves for my kitchen. I loved that garden
shop!

One spring day, I was browsing in the shop while

the clerk wrote up my order for some bedding plants. I noticed on a table that featured a number of sale items a dusty plastic bag full of something that looked like grass seed. The bag was not large, about the size of a pound of confectioner's sugar, and it had no commercial label, only a piece of paper glued to the plastic. The label read WILDFLOWER SEEDS. And under that title, handwritten, was this explanation:

> *These seeds are indigenous to this part of Connecticut. If you broadcast these seeds in a meadow, swampy area, or wooded grove, some flowers will grow. The flowers that grow will vary according to the season, sunlight, soil, and moisture conditions of the place they are planted. Only those flowers will grow that flourish in those specific conditions. The other seeds will remain dormant. However, it is guaranteed that wherever you broadcast these seeds, some flowers will grow.*

I was absolutely intrigued. In my imagination, I had already broadcast the seeds across the lower reaches of our front lawn, and I could see the results—flowers dancing in the sun, in all shades and varieties. I could imagine charming bouquets of wildflowers on my dining-room table, such a wonderful conversation piece, and another part of nature brought into the circle of our everyday experience.

I glanced again at the dusty little bag. The price tag was old and blurred, but it was decipherable: $1.98. How wonderful! A dollar and ninety-eight cents. Not much to pay for an experiment that could be so rewarding. I placed the bag next to my other purchases. "I'll take this, too, Jim," I said to the clerk.

He glanced up at me with a surprised look. "Are you sure, Mrs. Edwards?" he asked.

"Well, I know it's a bit of a gamble, and probably none of the flowers will grow," I answered, "but I figure it's still worth a dollar ninety-eight."

"Look again," Jim said, pointing at the label.

I looked again, and this time I saw more clearly.

"A hundred and ninety-eight dollars!" I gasped. "For this little bag? Why on earth would it be so expensive?"

Jim smiled. "It isn't easy to gather wildflower seeds," he said simply, "they are very rare and precious."

As I drove home without the wildflower seeds, I contemplated how much women are like wildflowers. We are each rare and precious, and when we are born, our nature is sown with dormant seeds. Talents, wisdoms, questions, characteristics, dreams, capabilities—all lie dormant within us as silent, fragrant possibilities. Each condition and season of our lives causes different seeds to sprout. Many seeds still continue to sleep, just waiting for the right conditions to bloom with unexpected beauty.

Who knows what will bloom within us during the open, sunny-meadow days of our lives? What quiet seeds lie waiting for the dark, shadowed, wooded days? Or what generous and hardy plant will suddenly sprout when our life turns into a treacherous swamp? Perhaps the darkest moment is when the most glorious flowers burst into blossom.

We once moved into a home in California with a garden planted with unfamiliar tropical flora. Late one night, having spent a long day doing laundry, tending a sick child, and trying to unpack boxes, I turned off the last light and prepared to go upstairs to bed. Before locking the front door, I opened it for a moment to take a deep breath of the cool night air. The moon was silver on the trees, but the night had a warm, dark feeling. I breathed deeply, and a sweet fragrance filled my lungs. The night seemed to sing with perfume, and I looked about me in wonder.

Next to the door, a plant that had hitherto escaped my notice, a rather straggly bush, had shot forth a tall, white stalk covered with blossoms. During the day, the stalk had looked like a green, knobby spike that needed to be pruned. But here, in the night, its green buds had opened and the white flowers were filling the blackness with a fragrance so sweet it was like a balm. The plant was night-blooming ginger, which flowers only in the darkest hours. During the day, it would merit scarcely a glance.

It is this unexpectedness in ourselves and in our lives that makes the revelations of mortal experience so precious. The discovery of truth and knowledge, the discovery of our own possibilities, requires that we be tested in every season, in every clime, in every condition. It is the only way that the dormant seeds within us will have the opportunity to flower.

Light from This Window:

൙ *We are like gardens sown with endless possibilities. We should not fear the changing seasons.*

Grownups never understand themselves, and it is tiresome for children to be always and forever explaining things to them.

—ANTOINE DE SAINT-EXUPERY
(from *The Little Prince*)

9

The Chair

I walked into the family room at four o'clock, the end of a busy afternoon. It was almost time to start preparing supper, the baby would need attention very soon, and in an hour I had to pick up Charles from his friend's house and drive children to music lessons.

The family room was a mess. Toys were scattered widely, and the floor needed vacuuming desperately. There was just enough time to accomplish the work. But I took a second look and sighed. How many times had I performed this same ritual? Suddenly it seemed a little pointless, more effort than I wanted to make.

On a whim, I walked across the room, sat down in the armchair, and simply stared at the disarray.

Just then my five-year-old daughter came through the door and crossed the room on her way to the stairs. She was heading for her bedroom with an armload of papers and crayons. She and her sisters were playing school upstairs and she had been sent out for supplies.

Intent on her errand, she walked right past me. Then, with one foot on the stairway, she did a perfect double take. She whirled, looked at me in disbelief, and came back to my chair and stood in front of me.

The chair was low, so our faces were level. She looked me directly in the eye with an expression of incredulity.

"Mother!" she exclaimed. "What are you doing sitting down?" The sight of me sitting down was obviously noteworthy to her.

The question startled me, and I answered facetiously, "Wishing I had a maid."

She did not laugh. She took my answer seriously, and cocking her head to one side, she thought about it for a moment. Then she climbed up on the arm of my chair. "Would you *really* like to have a maid?" she asked me in a direct, conversational voice.

I remember with great pleasure the discussion that followed. We sat side by side and talked seriously about housework, about my feelings toward home and children and work itself, and even about the concept of others working *for* us — or *with* us.

After a few minutes, she reached over and kissed me and said matter-of-factly that her sisters were waiting for her. I watched her go, and I felt refreshed and renewed.

How astonishing, I thought. *I not only have a daughter, I have just discovered a friend in my own house.*

Light from This Window:

෴   *Let your children see you sitting down
once in a while. You are much more
approachable that way. Don't always be a
moving target. Amazing things can happen
when you become still.*

Be our joys three parts pain!

Strive and hold cheap the strain;

Learn, nor account the pang; dare,

never grudge the throw!

— ROBERT BROWNING

10

Three Lessons from Pain

My favorite novel is *My Lady of Cleves*, by Margaret Campbell Barnes. In the final scene of the novel, Anne of Cleves is comforting Henry the VIII as he lies dying. She realizes that this monarch, who has been the most powerful man on the earth, is afraid to die.

"Henry," she says softly, "it has been my experience that the things we fear the most are often the things which come to happen. I have found that if we turn to meet them, and walk toward them with our head held high, we can walk right through them. And we are always better on the other side."

Never has a mother feared streets more than I did. My children were not allowed to cross streets by themselves until they were old enough to drive! Even then, I still preferred to hold my teenagers' hands and tell them, "Look both ways." My version of an ideal world was one in which children and cars *never* had to be on the same thoroughfare—sort of like a big block with everything on it, so no one ever had to cross the street.

I suspect it was inevitable, then, that *I* would be the one who would get hit by a car.

On a bright, sunny morning, out for a healthy walk, I crossed my street on a green light just as a young man in a big car decided to make a right-hand turn on his red light. I had seen his car stopped at the intersection and was sure he had seen me, but as I stepped off the curb, to my astonishment I saw the glint of something moving. I glanced back over my left shoulder. It was the hood ornament—and it was coming toward me!

In the next instant, the bumper hit my knee and I felt my leg explode beneath me. I fell under the car like a stone and lay there, pinned, as the turning wheel moved straight toward my head. By now I was fully aware that the driver had not seen me and was still unaware that I was under his car. A terrible death seemed certain. But then I heard his passenger scream at him to stop, and even though he did not know why, he stopped. I am so thankful for those seconds in which my life was surely spared.

As the ambulance carried me to the hospital, I began what would be months of operations, complications, disability, confinement, and profound pain.

There were many nights when, in the lonely darkness of my room, I wept to be spared the agony—to be able to find some relief. I watched precious time slip through my helpless fingers. I despaired of ever walking again. I chafed at my weakness and longed to be myself again.

Only slowly did I come to an acceptance of what I had been taught since childhood: that adversity brings strength, sorrow brings joy, and pain brings us the most priceless gifts. The value of something is often the equal of its price, so it is logical that the gifts of pain are infinitely precious—they are so dearly bought.

John Donne declared that we should never try to take others' tribulations from them. We would just as well rob the gold from their pockets.

I would like to share with you three of the lessons that pain taught me.

LESSON 1 ᕠ

Accept what is past and let it go. This lesson is perhaps the most valuable in a practical sense. It is the lesson I learned from a wise, dear friend, an immensely busy person, who had taken the time to come and sit beside me. From the depths of my pain, in that precious quiet moment of friendship, I felt free to ask her a difficult question, something that had puzzled me during the years I had known her.

"I'm not handling this experience very well," I said. "My feelings and attitudes are all wrong. May I ask you a very personal question? Since we have been friends, I have watched you go through many of the worst experiences possible—grave financial reverses, a dramatic change of lifestyle, challenges with your children, a death in your family. Through it all, you never change. You're always gentle, kind, generous with your home and your possessions, loving toward all whom you know, and faithful in your obligations. I *know* these things affect you deeply, yet you never show fear, anger, bitterness, disappointment, or gloom. I must know how you meet life with such steadfast faith and good cheer."

She looked at me for a long moment as she thought, and then she gave me a beautiful smile. "Jaroldeen," she answered, "whenever something difficult happens to me, I never question what has happened. I never ask questions that begin with *why*. '*Why* did this have to happen to me?' or '*Why* must I go through this?' or '*Why* would the Lord let this happen?' or '*Why* won't this go away?' or '*Why* aren't my prayers being answered?' I don't let myself worry about what can't be changed. All I worry about is 'What is my role?' and 'How does the Lord want me to act?' and 'What should I do?' and 'What can I do?' and 'What goals must I set to change this?' and 'What must I do to turn this into a building experience for me and my family?' "

As I listened to her, I realized that any growth that comes from pain and challenge can come only after we have stopped asking why. Growth begins when we have accepted what now *is* and what is *past*. Asking questions that begin with *why* is like racing the motor of our car without putting it in gear. What my friend taught me was reinforced by my son.

My college student son returned home many weeks after my accident. I was still very weak, restricted in my activities, and unable to walk. As he drove us past the intersection where the accident had occurred, I said, rather dramatically, "On that very spot, on June 21, my life was changed!"

"Don't do that, Mother," my son said gently.

"What?" I asked, surprised.

"Don't make a shrine out of it. Don't remember it that way. It gives it too much power over you."

He was right. The first thing we must do in order to begin to gain the lessons from pain is to accept what is past and let it go. Then we must begin to ask ourselves the *what* questions: What am I still able to do? What am I learning? What goals should I set?

The wonder of asking questions that begin with *what* is that it puts our life back in our own hands. We are no longer the victim of circumstances; we are now in control of our future. We have taken the reins of our free agency back in our own hands. Fear, anger, resentment, bitterness, confusion, and frustration only steal free agency from us.

LESSON 2 ∽

Another great gift of pain is *love.*

Pain is the catalyst that breaks the heart open and teaches the spirit to be contrite. As one's heart is opened, it can be taught the immensity of love.

Through trial, we may gain greater love for our family and a greater appreciation of their love for us. Even after all the years of serving my husband and my children and loving them as deeply as I thought it was possible to love, I have found that through the process of being served by them, I have gained a sweet and tender enlargement of my emotions.

Pain requires that we let those who love us serve us. In times of dependence, beautiful things occur.

On the night of my bone-grafting operation, my three daughters came to my hospital room. Because of my reaction to the medication, the room was kept bitterly cold. It was a very small, dreary private room, crammed with machines, tubes, bottles, and monitors. Heavily sedated, I could barely make out the faces of my daughters, two of them teenagers and the other a college student. They had each brought a light blanket or quilt, and all through the long night and the next day they remained with me, talking quietly, coming to my bedside at the slightest sound, sweetly encouraging me, and carrying on conversation even though I could not speak. Although my eyes were closed, I was acutely aware of their presence. It was immeasurably reassuring to me, more beautiful than I can say. I will never forget it.

Because of my injuries, I was unable to bend to reach my feet. They were rough, dry, and un-groomed, and I could not do anything about them by myself. It was a truly humbling experience for me to admit that I could not take care of my own intimate needs.

I suppose I had a hang-up about foot care; I felt it was a somewhat odious and private task, like brushing one's teeth. Anyway, it seemed an unpleas-ant thing to ask my husband to do, so I approached him with genuine feelings of reluctance and embar-rassment.

Of course, I knew Weston would gladly do any-thing I needed or asked, but I still felt it was some-thing that might be uncomfortable for him.

When I told him what I needed, his reaction was a lesson to me in pure love. He looked into my eyes with tenderness and gratitude and said, simply, "Thank you." Through those two words and his un-hesitating and heartfelt response, I suddenly understood that in my self-absorption with my pain and my sense of loss of self, I had been shutting him out.

He had been waiting patiently for me to reach out to him. There was nothing I could have asked of him—nothing that would have seemed ugly or imposing—nothing that he would not have welcomed as a way to be part of my experience, to be of help and comfort.

"Thank you" was all he said. Such a small incident—just two understated words said with unselfish generosity in response to my humiliating need—but I had never felt so much love or been loved so much in return. Love flourishes in shared need.

It reminded me of that precious phrase in *The Princess Bride* when Wesley, the farm boy, says, "As you wish" in answer to every unreasonable request of the princess. Finally, she asks him crossly, "Why do you always say, 'As you wish?' " and he replies, "It means 'I love you.' "

Through suffering, we gain an increased awareness of love for others. Suffering illuminates our hearts and minds and gives us a burning desire to help, lift up, and protect. Once harmed or hurt, we gain a great desire to care for others who are in pain.

LESSON 3 ∽

An important gift of pain is recognition of the need to cherish each moment. *Right now* is the best we have—it is *all* we have.

A friend called from Arizona to see how my recovery was progressing. "I was with a group of young mothers the other day," she told me during our conversation, "and they seemed to be so unhappy with their lives! They spoke of feeling trapped, overwhelmed, and overworked. One of them said, 'I get so tired of trying to fix supper with one child clinging to my leg and the other crying to be picked up.' "

I understood how those young mothers felt; I remember those feelings very well. But I also remember the feelings of enthusiasm, joy, and discovery—and the feeling that I was equal to the job of being a mother. I remember the feelings of zest and satisfaction in parenting much more vividly than the frustrations.

A sense of sadness came over me as I thought of those young women. Have we so failed today's generation of mothers that they see their children's preschool years as a punishment rather than a privilege?

I remember a precious day with my small son.

One day as I was driving five-year-old William home from kindergarten he looked at me with a sigh and said, "I've got to do homework today."

"What homework?" I asked.

"We have to do a report on an animal. Tell three facts. I've chosen polar bears."

"Great!" I said. "When we get home we'll get out the encyclopedia . . ."

This was beginning to sound like work to William. "I don't need the encyclopedia," he said firmly. "I already have my facts. Remember when we went to the San Diego Zoo? They told me all about polar bears, and I remember."

I decided to call his bluff.

"All right," I said. "What are your three facts?"

He began confidently. "Do you know why polar bears are white?"

"Why?"

"So they can blend in with the snow and their predators won't see them."

"Good," I said. "What's the next fact?"

"Do you know that polar bears have fur on the bottoms of their feet so they won't stick to the ice?"

This was a fact I hadn't known, so I applauded. "Good fact! And what's the third one?"

From the look on his face, I could tell he didn't have a third one, but the specter of being chained to an afternoon with the encyclopedia spurred him on.

"Well," he said after a little pause, "do you know why polar bears have *blue* eyes?"

This was a fact I was *sure* I had never heard. "No," I said. "Why?"

"So that," William said, thinking slowly and carefully, "when they dive into the water, they can open their eyes and it camouflages them in blue water and the seals can't see them and they can catch them." His smile was triumphant.

I looked him in the eye and shook my head, and we both started to laugh. To this day, I love the image of blue-eyed polar bears swimming around in the ocean with eyes wide open so no one can see them. Who would miss such a moment?

If we spend our life wishing away the mess, the noise, the obligations, they will be gone—but so will the children! This fact is true of every moment of life. If we do not see its joys, if we do not make the most of it, it will pass—and so will all of its opportunities.

I remember a day when I was a young girl, when my father came home early in the afternoon. It must have been a Saturday, because my brothers and I were home from school. Mother was at the sink, doing the dishes, and wearing a pretty apron with a big bow in the back.

Father came in and said, "Come on, let's drive up to Livingston and I'll show you the new ranch."

He had just bought a new ranch and none of us had seen it. It was about eighty miles away, up in the foothills of the Canadian Rockies.

"No, Charles," Mother said. "There's too much work to be done. I haven't finished the dishes and the children haven't done their chores. We have to shop and get ready for tomorrow. We just can't go."

Father went over to Mother, untied her apron, and, with a little laugh, twirled her around. Then he kissed her and said, "The dishes will wait."

We couldn't believe that Mother agreed! But off we went. We didn't even have time to change our clothes. We picked up cold cuts, bread, and fruit at a little general store in one of the small towns we drove through after we left the city, and by midafternoon, we arrived at the ranch property. We had not seen any signs of habitation for miles, only the great mountains coming closer, the lush green foothills rolling past and the dusty road winding between the long barbed-wire fences.

"This is where our property starts," Father said, waving his hand. "I think there's a stream beyond that little hill. Why don't we go down there to have our lunch?"

We grabbed the grocery bags and a blanket, squeezed through the barbed wire, and started up the hill. At the crest, we stopped in astonishment. The whole slope of the field as it fell away toward the sparkling stream was a blanket of wild tiger lilies, as crimson as a king's velvet robe. It was like coming across the poppy field in *The Wizard of Oz*. Such unexpected glory! Such treasured memories!

You will never hear a parent say with regret, "I wish I hadn't done so much with my children," or "I wish I hadn't spent so much time caring for my family," or "I wish we hadn't had so much fun together," or "I wish I hadn't loved them so much."

❊ ❊ ❊

It is through prayer that the blessings of pain can be perceived and realized. Many times during my recuperation, I wept, and the words of the children's song came unbidden to my mind: "Heavenly Father, are you really there? And do you hear and answer every child's prayer?" This song was sung by my grandchildren, and when they sang it, their mother sang in response in her loving voice, "Pray; He is there. Speak; He is listening." As I wept, I heard my daughter's voice in song, and her testimony lifted my faith, and I could pray.

And so I try to turn and face the hard things, to walk toward them with my head held high. I wish to remember the three lessons I have learned: accept what has happened and concern myself only with what to do now; let my heart rejoice in the renewed awareness of being loved and of loving; and discover and enrich each glorious moment.

Light from This Window:

∽ The lessons of pain are dearly bought but are doubly sweet.

I feel very strongly about putting questions;
You start a question and it is like starting
  a stone.
You sit quietly on the top of a hill;
And away the stone goes.

—ROBERT LOUIS STEVENSON

11
My First What Question

My tenth child was almost born on an airplane between New York and California. Weston had taken a new position in Los Angeles, and the plan was simple. He would drive the nine children across the country and get into our new house, while I remained behind in the East, had the baby, and then flew to join the family within two to three weeks.

Great plan. The only problem was, the baby had other ideas. Three weeks went by, the children were safely in Los Angeles, the furniture had arrived, but not the baby. I remained in New Jersey.

Finally, Weston had to report to work, so our two oldest daughters, young teenagers, were having to manage the family. Every night I would call. "What are you eating?" I'd ask.

"Oh, soup and junk" was the answer. (The soup sounded okay, but the "junk" was a concern.)

"Why only soup?" I asked.

"The stove isn't working" was the response. "We have to use a hot plate."

"We don't *have* a hot plate," I objected.

"We borrowed one from the neighbors," one of the girls replied cheerfully.

"What are you doing about keeping your clothes clean?" I asked.

"No problem," she answered blithely. "We just swim in our shorts and T-shirts and then the sun dries them."

At this point, I had an image of my poor, motherless children in wet clothes, barefoot, walking from door to door, begging for hot plates. I immediately decided that I would never be able to face our new neighbors. When and if I ever got to Los Angeles, we would just have to move!

The next day, I went to my obstetrician and begged him to write a note to get me aboard an airplane, since most airlines have restrictions against flying women in late pregnancy. He could see how desperate I was, so he said, "I think it would be all right. After all, you'll be in Los Angeles in five hours. What can happen in five hours?" He was an obstetrician and knew perfectly well what could happen in five hours.

No sooner had the plane taken off than I thought to myself, *It's nothing but indigestion.* A few minutes later I muttered, "Nerves. It's just nerves." Another few minutes, however, and I had to acknowledge what it really was. I was in labor!

I wish I could tell you my only concern was for the baby. And, in all honesty, I *was* very concerned for the baby, but my greatest worry at the moment was the fact that I felt I was about to be the star in a real-life documentary. I was seriously asking myself if it might be possible to have a baby on an airplane and not have anybody notice. However, giving up that line of thinking as futile, I stopped a passing flight attendant and whispered to her, "I'm having a baby." She sighed impatiently and gave me a look that said, *That's rather obvious.*

"No," I whispered. "I mean, I think I'm having the baby right now."

I'll give her credit for not dropping her tray, but she did lose her smile. She roared up the aisle, grabbed the microphone, and shouted, "Is there a doctor on board?"

Everyone on the plane stood up and stared at me, then began whispering. So much for anonymity. As it turned out, there *was* a doctor aboard the plane. She was sitting right next to me.

I was moved into first class with the doctor, and she sat and timed my pains as the plane continued to wing across the continent. We talked quietly; the pains continued, but did not get worse.

At last the captain announced that we were approaching the Los Angeles airport. We both heaved a sigh of relief. At about the same time, the pains stopped. "Probably the pressurized cabin," the doctor said.

I prepared to deplane, but was told to keep my seat until the plane was empty. The passengers filing by gave me very disappointed looks, as though they had been reading a book and hadn't been able to get to the last chapter.

After everyone had left the plane, four men in white leaped on board. Before I knew what was happening, they had me strapped to a hospital gurney and were wheeling me through the terminal.

I protested that I was fine and begged to join my husband and family, but they wouldn't listen or stop. You can imagine what a ten months' pregnant woman lying flat on her back on a gurney cart looks like!

My family had been at the gate, waiting for me to arrive in normal fashion—on foot. One of my children caught sight of me as I sped past, and she cried, "Mother, where are you going?" Then all nine children started racing after the gurney. Weston turned and joined the running procession in his three-piece suit, carrying his briefcase—but he was also trying to look like he didn't know who any of these people were!

As I was whisked into an ambulance, I called to him, "Find out where they're taking me and come and get me." The next thing I knew, I was speeding through the heart of Los Angeles, explaining to the medics that I was no longer in labor and watching palm trees whip by the windows.

At the hospital, the admitting clerk was very impatient. "Who is your doctor?" she asked.

I tried to explain that I had just arrived in town and had no doctor.

She stared at me, disbelieving, and angrily repeated, "Who is your doctor?"

"I am planning to call an old friend who practices obstetrics somewhere in the metropolitan area," I said. "But I have no idea what suburb he practices in. I was going to look him up."

"What's his name?" she snapped.

"Keith Merrill," I snapped back, having lost patience by now. "I'll call him as soon as you let me out of here."

Without a word, she wheeled me into a small examination room, closed the door, and left me.

By now I was thoroughly frustrated. "Please, Weston," I whispered to myself. "Find me and spring me!"

Just then I heard a voice over the hospital inter-
com: "Dr. Keith Merrill. Dr. Keith Merrill."

That did it. Hadn't anyone listened to me? I *told*
that woman I had no idea where he practiced. Why
on earth were they paging him?

Then the door opened and Dr. Merrill walked in
with a nurse. "I don't have a patient named Mrs. Edwards," he was saying in an exasperated voice, and
then he stopped and stared at me lying on the table.

We had not seen each other for more than fifteen
years, not since high school. "Jaroldeen!" he exclaimed. "Jaroldeen Edwards! What are you doing
here . . . and in *that* condition?"

I knew I had just been asked one of life's great
questions. It took me nearly two days of pondering to
come up with the true and satisfying answer. "Creating" is what I should have replied. "Creating a new
life. Creating a new home. Creating a wiser and better me." At that particular phase of my life, at that
time of frustration and uncertainty, hard work and
upheaval, discovering the answer to Keith's seminal
question gave me great peace of mind. Everything fell
into a meaningful place.

Since that day, I have thought of Keith's question
many times. I have found that if I can answer it to my
own satisfaction, I feel a touchstone sense of well-
being. When I start to lose my grip on who and what
I am, when life begins to lose its edge or fades into

something close to chaos or anarchy, I ask myself Keith's question. What am I doing here, and what is my condition? The answer, when I am able to think through to it, reimbues my life with a sense of purpose and worth.

Sometimes, when my life is off course, the answer brings me up short. I find that I am where I am for the wrong reasons or with the wrong attitude, or that I have wandered away from my real purposes. The answer to the question sometimes enables me to walk away from wrong choices when I ask, "What am I doing here?" and the answer reveals a lost sense of direction.

My daughter experienced the strength of this question when she pledged for a social club her freshman year at a university. One evening, in the midst of pledge activities, she overheard a remark made by a member of the club's pledge committee. "She's pretty enough and rich enough to be a good member," the young woman said, speaking of one of the potential candidates.

Suddenly my daughter asked herself, *What am I doing here?* She looked down at the items of clothing that she, as a pledge, had been required to wear. *And in this condition?*

The answer was clear to her. She was sitting in a place where values that mattered to her and goals that she felt were important were not well served. *I'm in the wrong place,* she concluded. She simply stood up and walked out. "I don't think I'm a good candidate for membership," she later told us with a smile.

On the other hand, the answer to Keith's question can sometimes give meaning to the most unexpected events.

One day I sat on a small kindergarten-size chair, with my knees up to my chin, listening to the rhythm band of my twelfth child's preschool group. It was really a dreadful performance, slow and out of tune. I had a dozen important things to do, and this little concert was not an important event, sort of a "come if you like" activity—a practice, actually. Only a handful of other parents had bothered to show up. I rubbed my aching back and thought that I could not even count the number of such concerts I had attended through the years. Who would remember? Not me, and probably not my children. Surely now, in my mature years, it wasn't necessary to attend everything.

As I squirmed impatiently in the little chair, I heard Keith's question pop unbidden into my mind. *What am I doing here?*

Just then my little daughter looked over at me and smiled. My answer to the question came, as solid and satisfying as the rock on which the wise man placed his house. *I'm building a child.* Suddenly the chair became comfortable and the concert seemed rare, precious, and fleeting.

Nothing in my life has been very predictable. I am consistently astonished when I pause to think about it. The places I have lived, the people I have known, the problems that have arisen, the opportunities that have opened, and the possibilities that have remained closed—all of these things are a source of amazement to me. But if I am in my spot, for the right purposes and in the right condition, all is well.

Light from This Window:

〰 *The right questions form the bedrock for the right answers.*

Love is enough,
though the world be a-waning.

—WILLIAM MORRIS

12
Niagara Falls

After seven years of marriage and five children, my husband finished his doctoral degree and we headed for the "real world." (The real world, in our case, was Chicago and a job with an investment firm.)

During those years, we had lived on Wright-Patterson Air Force Base in Fairborn, Ohio, and then in Harvard student housing—always in apartments. In the last months before Weston's degree was completed, I discovered we were expecting our sixth child, and I began to be impatient. I wanted to live in a real home.

The weeks seemed to drag as Weston finished his dissertation, and when at last, his doctoral committee heard his final arguments and the dissertation was accepted, I rejoiced—not only because of Weston's achievement, but also because it signaled my opportunity to finally have a house in which to live.

Weston was flown to Chicago, where he accepted a wonderful job offer. He also rented a large, old home in Wilmette. Then he flew back to Cambridge to gather us up in our old Chevrolet to make the trip to Illinois.

It was the dead of winter. The skies were gray and leaden, the roads treacherous, and our little car overcrowded. Our youngest child, who was then seven months old, was very irritable. She was recovering from an ear infection and had to be given medicine every four hours. She hated the taste of the bright pink liquid and persisted in spitting it up, so that everything in the front seat seemed to be spotted with the sticky stuff.

I know now that adding to the stress of the trip was my own mental attitude. I felt, deep inside, that I had waited longer than was reasonable to have a home of my own. The long wait had caused in me an intense yearning, a feeling of entitlement, almost an obsession, to get settled, to have space, stability, and the chance to create a substantial nest. Perhaps the best way to say it would be that I was *home*sick; that is, I was sick with the desire to be in my own home.

As the miles passed, I became increasingly eager to have the trip over. I wanted desperately to be someplace where I could begin to make a home. If I did not feel resentment, I certainly felt justified impatience.

When we neared Niagara Falls, Weston said, "I know it's winter, but I still think we should stop and let the children see the falls. They may never have another chance."

"No, please," I said. "Let's just keep going. The sooner we get to Wilmette, the better. I just want to get settled!"

"Dear," Weston said reasonably, "let's try to make this trip a bit of a vacation for the children. We won't have another break for a long time."

Late in the afternoon, we turned off the highway and drove through the deserted streets of Niagara Falls and out onto Goat Island. Except for the parking-lot attendant, we were the only people on the island. Weston parked the car near the entrance, where the lone attendant huddled in his heated booth.

The baby was crying. We were out of milk. The sun was beginning to go down. But with his infectious enthusiasm, Weston ran with the children across the empty parking lot to the viewing platform. There, in the bitter cold wind, they looked down on the ice-rimmed glory of the falls.

Soon they came running back toward the car, laughing and excited, their cheeks rosy with the cold. Weston insisted that I must go and look at the falls.

He took the crying baby, and, with great reluctance, I climbed out of the car and went over to look.

The sight was memorable, but as I came back, I looked at our car. Something didn't seem right. The luggage rack looked like a crazy hat tilting to one side. Then I realized the rear tire was flat as an airless balloon!

By now the three youngest children were crying. When he opened the trunk, Weston discovered that our spare tire was also flat. We caught the parking attendant just as he was preparing to leave, and he put in a call to a garage. Then he left for home. We sat, alone, in the vast parking lot, staring at the thundering falls as the sun set and night gathered in the surrounding trees.

It was almost an hour before we saw the flickering lights of a wrecker coming toward us. We were towed off the island and taken to a garage, where quick repairs were made. Then we hunted for a motel. The city of Niagara Falls is like a ghost town in the winter, with most motels closed, but we finally found a small establishment that had a vacant two-bedroom unit with two cribs. Obviously the motel was not expecting guests, for the room was dusty and cold. We did get the heat working, and Weston ran down the street to a diner and brought back hot soup, crackers, and milk. After feeding the children, I prepared to give them baths.

We had seen a drugstore a block away, and Weston said he would go down to it and get some more medicine for the baby. I was busy running water into the tub, so I called my thanks to him over my shoulder.

After I bathed the five children, I zippered them into their fluffy pajama suits. I tucked the older ones in bed and put the two youngest in cribs. One of the cribs was broken, and I spent some time figuring how to prop it up on some chairs.

The children were excited and restless, so we talked and I sang songs with them, and finally I told them a story. I turned off all the lights in the room, leaving just a tiny glow from the adjoining room, and lay down on the bed with them. One by one, they finally fell asleep.

As the room became quiet, I began to feel uneasy. Where was Weston? I didn't have a watch with me, but it seemed to me it had been well over an hour since he had left, and the drugstore was less than a block away.

I took a bath and prepared for bed. I expected him to walk in at any moment, but time moved slowly, endlessly, and he did not come. Finally I got up and got dressed again. I sat by the window and watched the road. There was very little traffic, and as a set of headlights would start down the block, my hopes would rise, only to be dashed when the vehicle moved on. The motel was in a run-down section of the city, and the streets looked dreary, deserted, and mean.

There was no phone in our rooms and I was terrified to leave the children alone, but by now, I was certain that Weston had been gone for over three hours, and I knew the drugstore was closed. I could think of no explanation for his absence. Fear had grown in me that something dreadful had happened to him. Maybe he had been mugged or had been in an automobile accident.

Finally I left the room, locked it, and went to the manager's office to ask if I could use his phone. He had been sleeping and was very curt. "No," he said, "guests are required to use the pay phone at the corner."

Since the pay booth was in view of our doorway, I ran to use the phone. It was bitingly cold and my voice was shaking with chill and fear. I found the number for the police department in the phone book and dialed. "Officer," I said, when a voice answered, "could you please tell me if there have been any automobile accidents or crimes reported in the last three hours? My husband left our motel room over three hours ago on a brief errand and he hasn't returned. I'm afraid something might have happened."

"Lady," said a bored voice, "does your husband drink?"

"No," I cried. "No. He is the most wonderful, responsible, caring man in the world."

"Well, there haven't been any auto accidents. That's all I can tell you."

As I walked back toward the room, I felt a heavy cloak of fear and worry, but piercing the weight of my terror was a sudden overwhelming realization of how precious my husband was to me. It was as though my heart was filled to bursting with the power of my love for him, my gratitude and joy for his strength and goodness, and the immensity of my need for him. I understood, perhaps for the first time, that everything good, sweet, and secure in my life came from and through him. Standing there in the dark, I had never felt my love for him more strongly—and I had also never felt more frightened and alone.

Just then a pair of headlights shone through the window, and I turned to see our car pulling into the motel. Weston climbed wearily out of the driver's seat.

"Where have you been?" I asked, tears streaming down my face as I opened the door.

With tenderness, he held me close. "Didn't you hear me?" he asked, astonished. "I called to you as I was leaving. I went back to the garage to pick up the other tire, and they hadn't even started working on it. I've never seen slower mechanics, but we couldn't leave tomorrow without a working spare.

I couldn't even answer him, I was crying so hard from relief and exhaustion.

"I'm so sorry," he said. "I couldn't phone you because there's no phone in the room. I just thought you'd know I'd run into a snag at the garage."

"I didn't hear you—the water was running," I managed to gulp. "I thought you were just going down the street for m-m-medicine."

We didn't say any more. More tired than knew, we lay down on the bed, and I cried until the warmth of his arms and the quiet of the room calmed my heart. Weston fell asleep, but I lay there beside him in that wretched, dusty room, in that alien city, with the lumpy beds, the broken crib, and the unknown world surrounding us, and I knew something that I have never forgotten. I was home.

Light from This Window:

❧ *We don't need walls or rooms or gardens or furniture or flowers or familiar scenes and neighborhoods in order to be home. Wherever those we love are, there home is.*

ᕲᕽᕒ

We do not ask for what useful purpose
the birds do sing,
for song is their pleasure—
since they were created for singing.

—JOHANNES KEPLER

ᕲᕽᕒ

13

The Blocks

Children have a refreshing way of looking at things, and many of the lessons I have learned as a mother have come from them.

We had moved to Connecticut and were building a house. In the meantime, we were living in a rented house with furniture and packing boxes stacked in the rooms and garage. It was a complicated time in other ways, too, with children in several different schools and needing chauffeuring at varying hours of the day.

Our oldest son, Charles, who had graduated a semester early from high school, had come to us and asked if he could work for our contractor on the construction of the house. Then he could feel that it was truly his home, even though he would be leaving soon for college.

My tentative grip on household organization

slipped further and further as the weeks went by. Things that normally seemed simple to me, such as getting the dishes done, the beds made, and the laundry folded, were suddenly monumental chores that had to be sandwiched between endless errands and unexpected demands. I felt as if nothing was under control. In the confusion, I began to lose motivation and let things slide.

My son came home every day for lunch. Sometimes he would have to fix his own, for I was often driving back and forth to the various schools or out looking at hardware for the new cabinets or some other item to complete our new house. This made me feel cheated, since I knew these few precious weeks were the last weeks I would have this wonderful young man at home.

One day I dashed in the door, with two of the younger children in tow, and saw him just finishing the peanut butter sandwich and milk he had fixed for himself. I had left the kitchen a mess. I hadn't even had time to finish the breakfast dishes, and the makings from the school lunches were still spread over the counters. It was demeaning to me to look at so much evidence that I was not handling my life well.

I sat down next to Charles with a sigh and asked, "Charles, do you think I've changed? I mean, as I'm getting older, do you think my personality is changing? I feel like I'm a different person."

For a moment, Charles thought, and then he looked me straight in the eye and said, "No, I don't think you're a different person. You see, I have this theory that everybody is born with a whole set of 'blocks' in their personalities—all different colors and shapes—but they each have their own individual set, and it's theirs for a lifetime. Then, as we live, we shape those blocks into a certain pattern, and for a time that pattern is fairly stable. Then something comes along, like adolescence or graduation—some big change—and it's as if all of our blocks get knocked down and we have to build up our 'person-hood' again.

"In a sense," he added, "I guess we change, because we usually build a new pattern—and maybe a new block comes out on top. But we are still building with the same basic blocks. So, in answer to your question, Mother, I don't think you've basically changed. I just think someone has knocked down your blocks."

Light from This Window:

တာ *Times of change and upheaval are invaluable. They give us a chance to redesign our blocks.*

The drift of pinions, would we hearken,
Beats at our own clay–shuttered doors.

— FRANCIS THOMPSON

14

The Desire to Remember

A few years ago I was driving my mother from our home in Connecticut to the John F. Kennedy Airport in Queens, New York. In order to get to the airport, you must cross the Whitestone Bridge. At the apex of the bridge span is a magnificent view down the East River to the tip of Manhattan Island. A dozen bridges span the river, and the graceful towers of beautiful Manhattan rise against the sky. I relish that view and always gaze at it as I cross the bridge.

My mother, however, was not looking at the view. She was staring speculatively at the intricate, vaulted trusswork of the bridge that spanned the sky over our heads. "My goodness," she murmured, "we have no comprehension of the debts we owe others."

Brought back from the view, I looked at her with

puzzlement. "What on earth are you talking about?" I asked.

"I'm talking about this bridge," she said. "Do you realize that we drive over this mighty structure without a thought? Who made it? What sacrifices and creativity were involved? What did each individual contribute? And . . . is it *safe?*"

We laughed at the progression of the questions, but she made me think about how casual we are about the debts we owe to others who have left the work of their hands and minds to enrich our lives.

Just think of the intellectual heritage represented by libraries; the spiritual heritage by scriptures, journals, and buildings; the family heritage in records, places, pictures, and inheritances; the unknown heritage of roads, bridges, trails, and cities. Maps, atlases, dictionaries, computers, television, radio, cars—all the heritage of those who have gone before.

Pursuing that thought, I decided to make a study of the Brooklyn Bridge in the year of the bridge's centennial. What incredible things I learned.

The Brooklyn Bridge was built by the Roebling family. The father, John, was a German immigrant who developed the concept of wire rope or cable, an invention that was necessary for the design of suspension bridges because it was essential to have a support system made of flexible strands that could bear tremendous weights.

In the first months of work on the bridge, John Roebling was standing on the dock when a ferry came up to the pier and crushed his foot. He believed in hydrotherapy and thought water could cure anything, so each day he bathed the foot in plain water and drank gallons of water. And he died a cruel death from tetanus.

After his death, his son, Washington Augustus, took over the construction of the bridge. Shortly afterward, he went down in a caisson one day to inspect the pilings. People did not understand the bends in those days, and so he was brought up too quickly and was disabled with what was called caisson disease. Nitrogen had invaded his joints, nervous system, and brain.

For the remainder of the time the bridge was being built, Washington remained in his apartment, which overlooked the building site, and watched progress on the bridge through a telescope by the window. From this vantage point he made suggestions, which his wife wrote down and took to the foreman. In reality, his wife was the moving force. Many people have speculated that the direction and ideas might have been her own, since Washington was so badly disabled.

The story is fraught with drama, tragedy, and heroism, and the bridge itself is like a cathedral, with its great Gothic stone columns and graceful necklaces of cables. A splendid walkway above the traffic lanes allows people to stroll or jog along the mile-long span, floating in the air high above the wide expanse of the East River. Such a legacy! And so symbolic of all the bridges left for us to cross and climb and reach new places. Their stories should be known.

The burden—and joy—of the past is that we must preserve it, learn from it, glean from it, and pass it on to the next generation.

Family stories should be known, told, and retold. One of my favorite stories of family heritage is of my grandmother, who was deathly afraid of water. Her own mother had drowned, and Grandmother had never learned to swim.

My grandparents, William and Ellen Russell, lived in Provo, Utah. In those days, a steamship took people on excursions across Utah Lake for a day of picnicking and fun; however, the lake was so shallow that passengers had to go out to the boat in a dinghy. One day my grandparents, with their new baby, decided to take one of these excursions. That day Grandmother wore a large hat, held on with netting, and a long, white dress with embroidery and a high, stiff lace collar. She was young, slender, beautiful— and very worried about going on a boat. Carrying her baby, who was also dressed in a long, white dress, she was lifted from the dock to the dinghy that would take them out to the steam paddler. As she was arranging her skirt to sit down, another passenger stepped into the boat and Grandmother lost her balance. Still holding the baby, she fell over backward into the water which was over her head.

Instantly Grandfather and some other men lifted her out of the lake back onto the dock. Dripping wet and in total shock, she stood on the dock, speechless. Someone tried to take the baby away so that they could towel her and the baby off, but they could not pry the baby out of her arms. Finally Grandfather gently loosened her hold and took the baby in his arms. The amazing thing was that Grandma had held the baby so closely and so protectively that the front of her dress was *bone dry*. Such love! What a wonderful heritage!

My husband's grandmother, Anna Rhodelia, was left a widow at the age of twenty-one. She had two little boys under the age of three and a third one was born four months after her husband's death. The family was destitute, living in a small log cabin and with no close relatives or friends.

When Anna's baby was born, Anna became terribly ill. She had a raging fever, had lost a great deal of blood, and was clinging to her life by a thread. A few relatives who visited her, seeing her in what they thought was a comatose state, began reluctantly to decide who should raise the children. None of them could take all three. Listening to them, Anna felt a great fire building within her, and she spoke directly to the Lord. "You have taken my mother and my father. You have taken my brothers and sisters. You have taken my husband. You must not take me. I must be allowed to live and raise my sons. I will not let them be raised without love—without one another."

Miraculously Anna rose from her deathbed, and through years of incredible sacrifice and work, managed to raise her three sons.

Within womanhood is magnificent power. We are descended from women who understood that power, and we must learn about them and teach their stories to our children.

America's Secret Aristocracy, by Stephen Birmingham, is a fascinating chronicle of some of the oldest, most aristocratic families of America, families that have quietly amassed and used power and wealth. These families form an unpublicized and private network, with subtle (and some not-so-subtle) speech patterns, mores, and traditions.

As I read his book, it was interesting to note that one of the traditions that keeps these aristocratic families cohesive is that they have a pattern of remembering their ancestry. Their homes are filled with family portraits, heirlooms, mementos of the past, and photographs. Their conversation is peppered with reference to their ancestors—eccentric, respected, and impressive men and women. Children are taught that the family's past is part of their present.

This is an example we should follow. As women, we have a unique, vibrant, and rich heritage that must be preserved. We should weave it into our daily lives and teach it to our children. It is the gold that we should garner from the ashes.

The more we know of the past, the better we understand the present. The more we know of others, the better we understand ourselves.

Ordinary women can do extraordinary things. Juliet Brier, with courage and undaunted will, led through the living hell of Death Valley a company of men who had faltered. Weighing less than seventy pounds, this amazing woman stood by Furnace Creek in the forgelike heat and declared, "Every step I take shall be towards California." She put her four-year-old child on her back and headed west. The others, men, women, and children, followed.

By her determination, she lifted the spirits of the whole group, and they struggled onward, becoming the first company of settlers to survive that journey. Such women should be remembered.

Light from This Window:

> We are the bridge over which the next generation will cross from the past to the future.

Often I am still listening when the
song is over . . .

—MARQUIS DE SAINT-LAMBERT

15

The Letter

᎒ D earest Marianna:

You are three years old today, almost four, and I have just given you permission, for the first time, to walk down our lane to your friend's house, five doors from ours.

The weather is cold. It is March, and, although most of the snow is gone, it has rained this morning, and there are some icy puddles of water in the lane.

When the phone call came inviting you to come for lunch, we went up to your room and you chose your favorite dress to wear. I wonder if you will re-member it. It is a rich brown cotton print, with tiny roses on it and a pretty lace collar. You put on white tights and the fluffy white crinoline that makes your dress puff out from its wide-bowed waistband. I had just polished your little white Mary Jane shoes, and you wanted to wear those, too. Then we put on your warm red coat and your white hat with the pompon. As I put the mittens on your hands, I thought how small and sweet they are. Your golden hair curls down your back and is almost long enough to reach the hem of your coat.

How dear you are to me! I am very worried about you walking to the neighbor's alone, but no cars are allowed in the lane, and each of the townhouses of Holden Green has its own door and stoop, so you have only to walk past five familiar doors and knock on the door of your friend's house. They are watching for you.

Still, it is very hard for me to let you go on your own. I wouldn't do it except that the baby is very sick and I cannot take her outside. Over and over again, I explained what you must do, and then I kissed you good-bye. The last thing I said was, "Your shoes are so white and clean. Please don't walk in the water and get them muddy."

The minute you left the door, I hurried to the window to watch until I could see you safely inside your friend's door. You had no idea that I was watching. You truly thought you were alone—on your own— and so you were. But I was watching, loving you, thinking how dear and precious you are, praying that all would go well.

At the first puddle, you paused, and I saw you

looking at it with yearning eyes. Such a lovely puddle! So perfect for splashing! I was certain that my last admonition would be completely forgotten.

Then I saw the most wonderful thing. With meticulous care, you skirted the puddle. On down the lane, with its dozens of puddles—big ones, small ones, irregular ones—you zigzagged, skipped, walked sideways, tiptoed, and did everything humanly possible to see that not one drop of water touched your polished shoes.

Never realizing you were being watched, you took your first step toward true independence. By your own choice, you obeyed with full heart the things you had been taught.

As I watched you, my heart nearly broke with love, admiration, and tenderness. And I thought that I must write this story down for you and give it to you now, on your sixteenth birthday.

You have become a beautiful young woman. As you continue your journey toward independence, as you begin to date young men and to prepare yourself for the great possibilities of your life, I hope that you will remember the little girl you once were and will follow her example. There will be many puddles and pitfalls that will tempt you, but if you are true to yourself, even when you think that no one is watching, that no one cares, you will arrive at your destination unspotted from the world.

You can do it, Marianna, for I saw you do it once, as a cherished, wise, and obedient three-year-old.

Thank you for the example and the joy you have been to me.

Love,
Mother

Light from This Window:

❧ *Keep the records of your life. For you and your family, they will become your own personal story.*

Out of our . . . lineage, minds will
spring that will reach back to us . . . to
know us better than we know ourselves.
(They) shall stand upon this earth
. . . and shall laugh and reach out
their hands amidst the stars.

— H. G. WELLS

16

The Nature and Privileges of Womanhood

I believe it is a magnificent thing to be a woman. It is a feeling I have had since I was five years old. I can remember watching my mother as she got ready to go to a formal dance. My three brothers and I were perched on her big bed, watching her add the finishing touches to her preparations.

Mother had been the chairman of the event and had spent most of the day at the ballroom supervising the final decorations and the placement of the banquet tables and organizing the program. Even her rushed and brief accounting of her busy day had about it the wonder of magical grownup events and the power she had to make splendid things happen.

As Mother put on the last touches of her makeup, I lay on my stomach on her satin bedspread and watched. She was wearing a black evening gown with huge puffed sleeves and a slender bias-cut skirt. At her neck was fastened her one ornament—diamond pavé clips. Her hair was shining black and she smelled of perfume and powder.

Last thing of all, she went into her closet and brought out her delicate silver sandals with the high heels. We used to play in the back of Mother's closet (we liked the way it smelled, like a hidden garden with roses and lilies blooming in the dark). I had seen Mother's beautiful shoes in their special box, but this was the first time I had seen her wear them.

Right there and then, as she put on the magic shoes, I was struck by the potency of womanhood—a palpable thing—so full of possibilities, from silver shoes to a silver tongue, from perfume to the fresh air on the high seas, from rocking a baby to scaling the flatiron rocks of the Rocky Mountains. There is such potential and power in womanliness itself, a fact confirmed for me when my father walked in, wearing a tuxedo, and looked at my mother with his eyes shining with admiration and love. We all sat spellbound in the unique influence of her femininity. It was something beautiful and spellbinding.

My feelings about my gender remain much the same today, after twelve children (eight of whom are daughters) and all the challenges of a long, complicated, and surprise-filled life. I am still exploring with wonder and gratitude that part of my identity that I prize so highly—the complex privilege and opportunity of being a woman.

Since our gender is an absolutely intrinsic part of our very existence, why should we be at odds with it? We should embrace the fact of it, value it, and help others to see it more clearly. Loving ourselves requires that we also love and cherish our identity as women, and the more we comprehend and value that role, the more we are able to comprehend and love ourselves and others.

Within the purview of the things for which women are primarily responsible—within the clasped network of our hands and hearts—are held the things that are the rewards and the foundation of any meaningful society—humanity, family, education, love, order, and nests. All these things are contained within the embrace of a woman's arms. It is rather a splendid armful. It is rather a splendid role.

I once saw a little painting at the art museum in Salt Lake City that depicted a pioneer mother with her two little daughters. The mother and children were standing on the prairies in the foreground of the picture, with the wagon train making camp in the distant background. The long skirts and hair of the woman and children were windblown. In a flood of golden sunshine, the little girls were filling their bonnets full of the bright sunflowers that carpet the prairie.

The young mother was smiling at her little daughters. Her face was so full of love that it almost hurt to look at her. The irony of the painting was that the mother had a wooden spade in her hands, and as she watched her daughters at their play, she was piling buffalo chips into a small wheelbarrow to take back to the camp for the evening fire.

As I looked at the picture, so full of beauty, duty, sacrifice, strength, and love, I smiled to myself and thought, *That's exactly what a woman's life is — sunflowers and buffalo chips.*

I am grateful for moments that make me see these things more clearly.

Light from This Window:

༺ *A book, a challenge, a friend, a child, a chore, a tale, a word, an act, a moment of stillness, a trial, a blessing, a prayer — all are windows into the light where we see ourselves.*

I never thought that you should be rewarded for the greatest privilege of life.

—MAY ROPER COKER
American Mother of the Year

17

Starfish for Breakfast

It was a hot, smoggy day in Pasadena and the children and I were getting a bit snappish.

"A day like this should be spent at the beach," I declared. Everyone was told to run and get on swimming suits and T-shirts and grab a towel.

We got into the family van with the bag full of beach toys that I keep in the garage, and the beach chairs were slung in behind with a couple of blankets.

That is all the preparation I make to go to the beach, since if it gets more elaborate than that, we take the whole day just getting ready to go.

That day was a pretty routine beach trip. I *never* take the freeway unless there is absolutely no other alternative. When I am going somewhere for fun, I take my kind of route, which means it must meander a little and go through towns and populated areas and not involve too much traffic or speed.

My husband laughs and says I have never forgiven the government for creating the cross-continental highways that bypass all the towns and cities. I used to love driving through the heart of small, forgotten, out-of-the-way places and stopping for a cold root beer at local family-owned drive-ins. Those days are gone forever.

However, I can still get around California on surface streets. So while the rest of the world takes the Santa Ana Freeway to get to the beaches of Orange County, I simply pull onto Rosemead Boulevard and head south.

About one hundred stop lights later, after driving for an hour and a half, versus the forty-five minutes the freeway would take, but enjoying every mile and every town and the company of each other in the air-conditioned van, we arrived at Seal Beach.

Seal Beach is an intimate oceanside community with a small, well-kept family beach and a lovely pier. It was crowded on that hot day with other mothers and children escaping the summer doldrums.

The waves were beautiful, and the sky grew blue as the sun reached its zenith and the morning haze burned away. In the afternoon, the sky was as blue as paint, and the children carried their buckets to and fro, building sand castles and forts and searching for the treasures left by the restless sea in the dunes and crevasses of the beach.

The sun skimmed their bodies (they were protected by sunblock) and polished their hair into spun gold. Sand dusted their rosy skin as though Midas had brushed across them with his charmed fingers, and they sparkled like the day itself.

When the time came to start back home, we were all replete with wind, heat, sound, and delight. Weary from playing with the whole of the sea, the children scrambled into the van, carrying their buckets filled with the treasures of their beach-combing.

We stopped at the corner Jack-in-the-Box and ordered huge sandwiches and drinks and gulped them down with the relish of deserved hunger.

Rosemead Boulevard seemed to be faster going home than coming, and, just as twilight began to lick at the ridges of the San Gabriel Mountains, we drove into our driveway.

My orders to the older children were brief. "Take everything out of the car, please. Put all the buckets and pails on the lawn. I don't want any of those sand crabs, seaweed, or other living items to come into the house. We'll sort everything out tomorrow."

The children piled out of the car, and the beach gleanings were placed in the carport. "Everyone have baths or showers and get ready for bed," I called. "I'm going up to bathe the little ones."

So saying, I gathered up my four youngest and headed for the big bathtub in my room, where I stripped off their sandy suits and popped them into the bath and washed them, shampooed them, and then lifted them, dripping, from the tub.

I could hear my other children downstairs. They were laughing and talking and there was a lot of whispering and running to and fro. Occasionally I called down to them to hurry with baths and bed, and they called up that they were going to be "just a minute."

By the time I had settled the four little ones into their beds in clean pajamas, with a bottle for the baby and stories for the others, it was dark outside and I was exhausted.

The older children were all in their rooms by then and the lights were off downstairs, so I went from room to room and bid my tired crew good night.

Weston was away on a business trip, so I went straight to bed—as tired as the children—and the house settled down to the sweet silence that follows a day of happy fun.

Early the next morning, I woke with the dawn streaming through the windows of our bedroom. Not one of the children had awakened yet. I knew the vigor of their day at the beach would ensure that most of them would sleep late, so I slipped out of bed, thinking that I would go downstairs and sort out the buckets they had brought from the ocean.

The shells I would clean and keep, but everything else was probably perishable and would need to be thrown away.

Walking down the stairs in the silent, morning house, I had such a sweet feeling. The warm happiness of the day before seemed to linger in the air, and I thought how satisfying it had been to change a day that had been tense and pointless into one of summer activity and family closeness.

As I entered the kitchen, I was assailed by a briny odor. Astonished, I turned the corner and walked out into the patio dining room where we always ate breakfast.

There, to my astonishment, I beheld a remarkable feast. The table was completely set for breakfast. The table center was a beautifully arranged bucket full of seaweed and driftwood, with shells tastefully placed around it.

There was a place set for each of the twelve children and one for me at the head of the table. Each plate had a fork, knife, and napkin beside it, and on the plates were placed the booty from our day at the beach: on one plate, a partial lobster tail; on another, a small, artfully designed cluster of sand crabs; on another, shells surrounding a seaweed roll; and so on.

It looked like the sampling table from a gourmet restaurant.

It was a splendid prank. As I looked at each ingenious plate — tantalizing despite the pungent smell — I could not believe how resourceful the children had been. I could imagine them as they came up with the idea, whispering and urging one another on until the joke had flowered into something unique and inventive.

All this work, all this creativity, all this delicious secrecy, just to make me smile, I thought. And it did. It made me smile from inside out, from top to bottom.

Such a delightful, intimate, unexpected moment as I stood there in the rosy dawn in that sparkling room and looked at a masterpiece of inventive love.

Then I looked at my plate. At the head of the table, surrounded by a bed of kelp, sat the treasure of the day. It was a dead starfish that the children had discovered in a clump of driftwood. They had thought that finding it was a triumph, and now it sat, squarely in the place of honor, in the middle of my breakfast plate.

You may say what you will about raising children, and I probably won't contradict you. Yes, there are times that it is hard, discouraging, and long, but the one thing I know is that it is the only profession in the world that has power breakfasts that are served with starfish as the main course.

Moments such as this, each as rare and unique as an island, stand alone in their own instant of time. They cannot be replicated or foreseen. They are the priceless, unexpected gifts that startle our lives with jolts of joy—like walking on an ordinary beach on an ordinary day and suddenly finding a perfect sand dollar.

It seems to me: if we believe in what we are doing; if we try to love and care for the people around us; if we fill our days with the best of what is in us and work hard; if we learn to recognize and treasure what is wonderful and let the rest have no power over us; if we love children and beauty and this great flawed world, we will have these brief moments when everything will come together in a sweet and perfect harmony and in a sudden glimpse we will know it is all better than we could ever have imagined.

If we are wise enough to see them, such moments will be there.

Last year my husband was in the hospital for emergency surgery. Many of our children were married, or away at college, or struggling with their own challenging lives. Within hours every one of those children had either come home, called, or reached out their hands. "Whatever you need. Whatever we can do. Whatever you want. We are here."

In as tight a circle of love as the one that bound our table on that starfish morning, our children were still there for us, and I realized that somehow in all the struggle and sweetness of our family's years together we have created something that will yield moments of precious joy for as long as our hearts can feel.

Light from This Window:

෴ *Sometimes we just turn a corner, and the unexpected reward is there, waiting. The walk is worth the surprise. Those who love may find starfish for breakfast.*

About the Author

JAROLDEEN ASPLUND EDWARDS is the mother of twelve children, and her husband, Dr. Weston Eyring Edwards, a Harvard graduate, is a distinguished business consultant. The Edwards family has lived in Chicago, New York City, Dallas, and Boston and is currently residing in Orange County. Mrs. Edwards, who has published six novels as well as works of nonfiction, is also a lecturer and speaker. She is an active volunteer in the elementary schools and is deeply concerned with issues of family, parenting, and education. She also loves music, history, books, and fun.